WE MIGHT AS WELL WIN

WE MIGHT AS WELL WIN

*On the Road to Success with
the Mastermind Behind
Eight Tour de France Victories*

JOHAN BRUYNEEL with Bill Strickland

Foreword by Lance Armstrong

Houghton Mifflin Company BOSTON NEW YORK
2008

www.houghtonmifflinbooks.com

Library of Congress Cataloging-in-Publication Data
Bruyneel, Johan.
 We might as well win : on the road to success with the mastermind behind eight Tour de France victories / Johan Bruyneel
with Bill Strickland ; foreword by Lance Armstrong.
  p. cm.
 Includes index.
 ISBN 978-0-618-87937-3
 1. Tour de France (Bicycle race) 2. Sports — Psychological
aspects. 3. Bruyneel, Johan. I. Strickland, Bill, date. II. Title.
 GV1049.2.T68B79 2008
 796.6'20944 — dc22   2007043921

Book design by Melissa Lotfy

Printed in the United States of America

MP 10 9 8 7 6 5 4 3 2 1

Cover photograph of Johan Bruyneel copyright © Walter Iooss
Styling by Lori Modugno; grooming by Landy Dean; clothing
courtesy of Earth, Wind & Rider; bike courtesy of Trek

TO MY FATHER,
my first and only hero

TO MY DEAR MOTHER,
for being proud of me

TO LANCE,
a true friend through good and bad

TO MY WIFE, EVA MARIA,
thank you for always being there,
supporting me, understanding me,
advising me, and above all, loving me

AND TO MY DAUGHTER, VICTORIA,
my biggest win in life, who makes
me feel so fulfilled and from whom
I'm learning every single day
what real life is about

CONTENTS

Part III: Putting It All Together

FOREWORD

IT'S SIMPLE: I wouldn't have won one Tour de France without Johan Bruyneel, let alone seven in a row. Johan is a Belgian ex-racer who was my team director during that winning streak, but that doesn't begin to describe him. He became my friend, the closest thing I've ever had to a brother, my confidant, my partner in obsession, and the greatest coach not only in cycling but all of sport. He's a genius—not necessarily a schoolbook type of genius, but one whose intuition and street smarts are unrivaled.

But the first thing he did for me, the one thing that made everything else possible, was at once the simplest and probably the most difficult for people to do: he believed in me.

After I was diagnosed with cancer and was trying to make a comeback in professional cycling, Johan was the first person who told me I could not only return to the sport but win the Tour de France, the biggest and most important bike race in the world. This wasn't some kind of motivational trick or complex psychological strategy. Johan looked deep into me and understood something. And whatever he saw changed my life.

Once I believed in his belief and we began working closely together, I discovered that he is one of the few people alive who might be more obsessed with winning than I am. I was obsessed with racing, training, equipment, recovery, and rest. He was focused on all of that—for twenty-five riders—plus figuring out what races the team should do, what our travel schedule would be, what we should eat, who should room with whom, which riders on other teams we would need three years later. He's the poster child for winning.

No one can argue with his record—in nine years of contesting the Tour de France he won seven times with me and once with Alberto Contador, in 2007. Phil Jackson, John Wooden, Vince Lombardi—they're phenomenal. But no one has a consecutive seven-time championship record at this level, or anything near an eight-times-out-of-nine record—not in the NCAA Final Four, the Super Bowl, you name it. I mean, I had to pedal the bike, but he called 80 percent of our shots. Now that I'm retired and I've ridden in the team car with him, following the racing pack, I've gotten to see the race from his side—and I'm even more astounded by his instinct for victory. There's so much more going on in the team car than you can imagine. You're trying to formulate your strategy and gather information about the race while listening to a race radio and reports coming across in about five different languages, and you have to get water bottles or food up to one of your riders, or get someone with a flat tire back on the road, but you can't let your attention waver from the simple task of driving or you'll run over someone. You can kill a guy if you don't drive straight.

Meanwhile, because you're following the pack or stuck in a certain place, you can't really see the race, you can't see the faces of the other racers or competitors. You have to rely on the information your team's riders are sending back to you, and you have to filter everything through what you know about them: are they tired, are they only seeing part of the race, do they know what you know about the upcoming course—it's an environment few people would be able to drive safely in, let alone muster the brain power to implement a victorious strategy.

And, like any true winner, Johan made it look easy.

It was never easy, of course. Winning never is. In 2000, the first year I was a defending Tour de France champion, Johan and I spent the spring all alone and all over France, practicing some of the climbs that we knew would be key to that year's race. While

I rode, he would support me, enduring hour after hour of driving a car at 20 mph. No one else was crazy enough, or committed enough, to help me study and conquer each road.

One time in particular stands out for me still. It epitomizes everything Johan and I were about. On a cold, wet day we came to Hautacam, a ski slope in the Pyrenees that streaks upward for nearly eight miles. It was slated to be that year's first mountain stage. As rain, then snow and sleet slashed down on us, I rode up the mountain. Johan and I tried out various places to attack. I got out of the saddle at certain corners while we tried to judge if that was the best place to attempt to gain an advantage. We tried to figure out where to conserve energy and where to spend it for maximum effect. I climbed for about an hour in weather so bad all either of us wanted was to be in a nice, warm room somewhere.

He was in a car, but it's not like he was basking in comfort. He kept sticking his head out the window into that driving rain. The wheels slipped and slid. He was aching from sitting so long. He'd given me the best, most nutritious food we had. But more than that: he was there with me. I knew instinctively and deeply that he'd have been out on the bike with me if that was what it took to win. Instead, we needed him in that car, taxing his mind as rigorously as I was thrashing my body.

At the top, Johan pulled the car beside me and stuck his head out the open window once more. His dark hair was plastered against his forehead. Water ran down into the cleft in his chin. "Well?" he said. "Good? Get in and let's get some hot tea."

I shook my head and said, "I didn't get it."

"What do you mean?" asked Johan.

"I didn't understand the climb," I said. "It's not my friend. Let's do it again."

It was crazy. I was crazy. We were cold and tired. We'd already studied this horrifically steep mountain in more detail than any professional racing team ever had in history. No one else on earth would have told us we needed to do the climb again. And, to be honest, I'm not sure that either of us would have even considered such a thing if we were not paired together. I drew inspiration from him, he drew determination from me. I could always count on the fact that Johan understood that, to win, we needed to go beyond what was reasonable.

To me, it's not so remarkable that we did Hautacam all over again. What sticks out in my mind about Johan is that, without one further question we turned around and descended the mountain for thirty minutes, then pointed ourselves back to the peak and spent another hour in misery going straight back up.

When the Tour de France started that year, I took the yellow jersey on Hautacam. That was the glory. But the victory really happened out there in the driving rain and sleet. That was Johan and me. Whatever it took to win. Without question. With absolute belief. And with a kind of closeness that is found so rarely—too rarely.

I love winning. But I just might love Johan Bruyneel even more.

LANCE ARMSTRONG

PROLOGUE

"We Might as Well Win"

*If you're going to expend that first big block of effort
and energy to participate, you might as well go ahead
and give whatever else it takes to win.*

WHAT WAS IT LIKE?
That's one of the two questions I get asked the most.
The first thing most people want to know when they find
out what I did for a living—and who I did it with—is: What was
it like to work with Lance Armstrong, cancer survivor, hero, seven-
time Tour de France champion, greatest athlete on earth? The answer, as with most of the answers I've found in life—and in the
Tour de France—sounds deceptively simple.

Imagine, I tell people, you're standing in line to board a groan-
ing city bus one day when someone plucks you up and plops
you into the cockpit of a rumbling, roaring fighter jet. Or imagine you're invited to play a game of chess but when you sit down
you realize that your king is some sort of unprecedented, one-of-
a-kind phenomenon that, rather than needing to be protected and
sheltered to win, will be able to launch blistering offensive attacks
by leaping squares faster and farther and in different ways than
any chess piece ever has.

People understand what I'm trying to tell them: Power. Adrena-
line. Force.

But most people also miss the second half of those analogies

—which is the important half, if you're interested in anything more substantial than simple thrills. Put a civilian in charge of a fighter jet and you're more likely to end up with a smoking wreck than a decorated and glorious hero. Give chess novices a super-king—give them two, or three—and the board will still be ruled by a grandmaster opponent who has studied hundreds of thousands of games and memorized every opening and endgame and plays ten moves ahead of ordinary comprehension. Muscle power without mental power means nothing.

People—mostly insiders who understand the sport of cycling and the intensely symbiotic relationship between team directors and star riders—also ask the all-important second question: Could you and Lance ever have won if you'd not met each other?

There's no simple answer at all for that. Lance Armstrong and I found each other at the perfect time. We'd each had some success when we met but neither of us had really found our specialty, the thing that would take us to the top of our sport and our particular potentials.

In 1998 I was thirty-four, freshly retired from a twelve-year pro racing career whose highlights—I won two stages of the Tour de France, and once wore the yellow jersey given to the race leader —arose more from cunning and tactics than from sheer physical ability. I had the mind and heart of a champion, but not the engine; at my best, I could sometimes beat the best, but the hard truth was that winning the Tour de France was simply beyond my physical capabilities.

I'd been racing since my teens, and wasn't sure exactly what I wanted to do. I'd always felt, from the time I was a child, that my destiny was to be a great champion of something, but my career had shown me otherwise. I wasn't disappointed in what I'd done, but I wasn't fooling myself either. In one sense, I'd accomplished great things—risen to the most elite level of bike racing, ridden alongside great racers and colorful characters, and lived a country-hopping life that aspiring cyclists dream of. I'd gotten new bikes every year, and uniforms, and clothes to wear, and all the food and other perks that enabled me to live comfortably. To those who'd tried to become a pro at that level but failed, I was living the dream. I knew that. I appreciated that. But in another sense I was also aware that I hadn't left my imprint on the sport the way I'd dreamed of doing when I was a kid.

I had half a thought that I might try to head up the pro riders' union, which at the time was weak, unorganized, not really an advocate for the athletes. I knew that someone needed to show the riders how, if they could all just band together and take a tough stand, they could quickly accomplish things such as raising salaries at the low end (where, after years of sacrifice, a rider sometimes makes just into five figures), securing better contracts with more guarantees, improving the insurance options. They were all important issues, issues that would leave a mark on the sport. But not in the way I wanted.

I also knew that I could go into sports marketing for some team, or help promote a race series. I'd studied marketing back in Belgium, when I was still racing as a young amateur. I loved the way ideas could be brought to life and communicated to people, the way a good marketer could bring excitement to any subject. There was something about the logical, methodical flow of progress from an idea's conception to its presentation to the public that appealed to me. And my facility with languages—I spoke five fluently, ripping through courses in school thanks to a natural affinity—would help get any message across in any country in Europe, which is the hotbed of pro cycling.

Either of those two options seemed like the natural next step. And yet, something held me back from committing to them. I knew it was time for me to retire but I also had this sense that if I abandoned the competitive part of cycling I would feel for the rest of my life as if pro cycling had somehow gotten the better of me.

And I hate losing more than I love winning.

It seems funny now that I gave no thought to the idea of being a team director—a position most often compared to that of a baseball manager or basketball coach, but which is really more like being a CEO and coach at once. Yes, of course you choose the lineup, create the game plan for the season and each race, call the plays, and organize, implement, motivate, and discipline the athletes. But you also manage the staff the fans don't see — the board, the assistant team directors, the mechanics, the massage therapists, the doctors, the office managers, legal counsel, public relations staff, and even a bus driver and a chef. (For our U.S. Postal Service and Discovery Channel teams, it was a support staff of as many as forty, in addition to up to twenty-eight riders.) It's not that I didn't want to be a team director; I just never thought of it. Why would I? Who would hire me? I had no experience.

Even if I'd had experience, I probably wouldn't have put Lance's team (which was then U.S. Postal) at the top of my list. They were, as Lance himself once described it, "the Bad News Bears, a mismatch of bikes, cars, clothing, equipment." The team's total budget was $3 million, less than the salary of some of the world's best racers.

And Lance, himself — well, he was not yet LANCE, the one-word beacon of human potential, hope, and triumph that he's become. He already had the obsession, and the drive, and the physical ability that's led him to greatness. But it hadn't all gelled — and there was no way it could have by then. He was twenty-seven, still a child in terms of experience in the peloton, which is what a pack of pro cyclists is called. He'd shown enormous promise as a one-day racer (winning a world championship at age twenty-one, and two stages of the Tour de France) before being struck by cancer, but his comeback was a patchwork of failures (dropping out of races) and near misses (finishing fourth in the Tour of Spain, a late-season stage race). He was not a Tour de France champion. He was an experiment.

We were opposites in many ways. I'm from a big, happy family in cycling-mad Belgium, where biking, second only to soccer in popularity, is shown on national TV nearly two hundred days a year, where no matter where you live there's a nearby race just about every day of the week that attracts thousands of spectators, and where from their teens promising riders are adopted and nurtured by local fans and coaches who buy their equipment and pay their expenses. From nearly as early as I could remember I'd been surrounded by bike racers and wanted to be one of them, the way nearly all American kids want to be basketball stars at some point in their lives. In my family, in my neighborhood, we rode more often than we didn't over the course of a week, and there were at least a couple local races each weekend and many through the week as well. The speeds were fast, the corners tight, the roads were in horrible condition, and the rain and wind were our constant opponents.

I was gifted enough physically to find success as a kid. I became a local star, then, as a teen, a regional power and a threat at the national level, and eventually, in my twenties, I found out that I had what it took to ride among the best in the world. It felt almost like a career track — in Belgium, you were lucky and gifted and determined if you made it as a pro cyclist, but you were not by any means an anomaly; it was what Belgian athletes became.

Once I began competing against other world-class athletes, however, I quickly realized that I could not dominate races the way I'd done back in my neighborhood, racing against my friends and kids I'd known all my life. But I found out that I could steal a win here and there by racing with my head as well as my heart. I became a sponge — soaking up the impressions and subtle clues riders gave off about their form, learning more about my opponents than they sometimes knew about themselves, studying course profiles, planning meticulous strategies for single races, and embracing both the nuances and the deep core truths about the curious and mysterious sport of cycling.

For instance, when two riders jump ahead of the pack and break away on their own, they must cooperate — each taking turns at the front to block the wind, saving energy for the rider in back so that together they have the strength to hold off the charging pack. But as the pair approach the finish line, at some point they must turn on each other; the very rider you've depended on for survival, cooperating like brothers for miles and miles and hours and hours, instantly becomes your most bitter rival and you try desperately to leave each other behind—but not too soon, or the pack will catch you as you struggle solo to the finish.

The strategies used to win a bike race, especially a multiday stage race as opposed to a one-day event, are shockingly simple, and not all that numerous. For instance, once you have a day where you gain some time on your chief opponents, you no longer have to beat them on the following days; you simply shadow them so you do not lose time. The leader wins by being led. There's no way around that, and your opponents know, so they must attack you, trying over and over to ride away. It's no secret. Another example: if you're behind in time, you send your second-strongest teammate to the front to attack before you do; if he is successful and rides away from the group, he tries to gain enough time to threaten the leader's top position, which means the leader must then stop following you and attack—making him vulnerable to fatigue, and to your own attack that will come later. Or, if your teammate gets away but doesn't gain much time, he might soft-pedal, waiting patiently far up the road. When you attack, dragging the leader (who is doing the right thing by following) along with you, you will at some point meet up with your teammate; the two of you can then take turns attacking the isolated leader.

Everyone in cycling knows and understands these few strategies. The difference is that amid the chaos and speed of a bike race, only a very few people in the world are able to execute them consistently, and at the right time. Only a few people are able to block out the madness of a bike race and focus on the fundamental strategies, while still being able to remember everything about the course profile or keep in mind a subtle clue an opponent might have given about his condition that day. So even at its most basic level, though cycling strategy is simple, the sport has no element as uncomplicated as throwing a ball through a hoop to score a point. I reveled in these complexities, and learned how to ride alongside cyclists who were much more talented than I.

Lance, famously now, grew up with unstable or absent fathers, roughing out life with his mother, who raised him as a single parent and sacrificed much to give him what little they had, in a country where the general public considers the bicycle more of a child's toy than a high-tech marvel of sport gear.

Where I was part of a long tradition when I began racing as a kid, he was an exception. And he won races differently, with raw horsepower and guts. He cared little for the traditions and unspoken rules of the peloton.

But in the few years we raced against each other, I as the aging insider and he as the brash kid, we'd improbably shared some key experiences—moments of intense beauty and agony—that forged an unlikely bond. By 1998, when I was retiring and Lance, who was searching for something, asked me to become his team director, it was perfect timing for both of us.

As soon as I realized I had a chance to be Lance's team director, I understood why I'd been hesitating about my other career options. It crystallized for me: I didn't just want a job. I wanted one last chance to become the champion that racing had both shown me I could be and kept me from being. Here was my chance— the opportunity to become the best team director in the best race on earth.

The Tour de France is the greatest sporting spectacle because it transcends bicycle racing. The Tour de France is like life. It's not a game, or a series of games. It's a two-thousand-mile, month-long odyssey that creates and breaks heroes, elevates some while diminishing others. There's unspeakable triumph and heartbreak, not in fleeting moments but washing over you for sustained periods. There are disasters, and illnesses. Babies are born while racers speed simultaneously away from and toward home. Deep friendships develop. Rivalries, too. Bikes crash. So do cars. There are cheaters—and there always have been, though the methods have varied. The Tour de France is the only sporting event, someone once said, so long that you have to get your hair cut in the middle of it. This messiness and glory is what I think of when I say the Tour de France is like life itself. It was always where I had most desired and most sought to prove myself.

Everything I knew about cycling, and about the Tour, was telling me something about Lance, this kid who'd been a spectacular one-day racer but had never even finished a complete Tour de France, and who was trying the most improbable comeback in all of cycling, if not sport. I turned off my brain and listened to my heart.

I accepted the job. Then I told Lance something shocking.

"I think we should focus on the Tour de France," I said.

"Okay," said Lance. "Which stages? I can win a few stages."

"No," I said. "I want to see you on the podium. I want to win the whole thing."

Lance said nothing for a moment. Years later he would tell me, "I thought it was far-fetched, but at that point I had nothing to lose."

"Look," I said. "If we're going to ride the Tour, we might as well win."

Finally, Lance said, "Sure. Okay, let's do it. Let's win the Tour de France."

We might as well win. I've always had this idea that if you're going to try something, if you're going to expend that first big block of effort and energy to participate—whether it's riding the Tour de France or applying for a new job or coaching your daughter's soccer team—you might as well go ahead and give whatever else it takes to win. I mean, I'm going to be there no matter what, right? Why not go ahead and get the victory?

It's a simple idea—but it's one of those simple ideas that, like cycling itself, or like trying to explain what it's like to work with Lance—is full of hidden meanings and finer points.

Over the course of the seven years Lance and I contested and won the Tour de France together—from 1999 to 2005—then during the year after Lance retired, when I didn't win the Tour, I absorbed a life's worth of wisdom about what it takes to win, and how to learn to win from losing.

The Tour de France became my crucible. I emerged from it as the most successful team director in history. I don't think you can become a winner, or figure out how to turn loss into victory, through some snazzy ten-step program full of catch phrases and bullet points. I think you have to immerse yourself in life, in the race, in the stories, in the experiences of triumph and failure. I think you have to absorb it, not memorize it. And I think we all have such chances in our lives; every day we deal with the elements of success and failure. Every day we bump into people who can help us or hinder us. Every day we are given a choice to attack or follow. Sometimes it's hard to figure out what to do, or to know if you're doing the right thing once you're doing it.

All I know for sure is that winning starts with belief. It's the one thread that runs through every story in this book, the one constant in my life: no matter what the experts said, no matter what the facts seemed to indicate, no matter which way I was being pushed, by money, or the media, or fans, I made every decision with my heart, and once I made a decision I committed to it all the way. I made decisions as if I were jumping off a cliff. I didn't want to leave any possibility for second-guessing.

That's not to say I leapt into those decisions blindly; I didn't want to fall to the ground and die. I wanted to jump, then soar. Leaping off a terrifying cliff takes heart. To fly instead of fall, you better have been smart enough to build a glider—or a jet—before you jumped. (Or possess the quick-wittedness to put one together on your way down.)

This is not an autobiography, nor is it a comprehensive chronology of every Tour de France I won with Lance and Alberto Contador. This is the expression of the moments that stick with me, the simple yet somehow profound stories about how I won and lost—and won again, thanks to all that I'd learned from Lance, from the Tour de France, from bike racing, from my father, from my team, and from the ticking of my own heart.

WHAT I LEARNED FROM WINNING

1

Follow Your Heart — But Bring Along Your Head

I had, for the first time, hooked my heart and my head together and, in the alchemy of that combination, created something more powerful than the parts.

N 1993 I PERFORMED A MIRACLE.

Or maybe I was granted a miracle. To this day, I'm not sure which. I know this: it was the first time I rode with each element it takes to win a bike race — my body's physical ability, my mind's acuity, and the passion of my heart — fully integrated and working together seamlessly. I rode for one magic, tragic day with everything I was.

After years of proving my mettle first with amateur teams in Belgium, then with smaller pro teams, I was in my second season with the Spanish team ONCE, a top-notch squad that regularly fielded Tour de France contenders and featured champions such as Laurent Jalabert and Alex Zülle (who at the end of the decade would battle Lance for the Tour de France crown).

On such an exalted team, my spot in the hierarchy was clear: I was not a champion. I was not a superdomestique, either — one of those riders whose career exists only as a sacrifice to the team's leader. I was something in between. I was a threat to win stages of the Grand Tours (the three major European stage races, including the Tour de France and the tours of Spain and Italy), and some one-day races, but my true value seemed to be as a kind of rolling strategist. I had a knack for reading races and racers, and intuiting what the winning moves would be. On the road, I was like a radar antenna, casting my attention across the entire field until I picked up some useful impression: someone's pedaling style looked a little ragged that day, or something seemed slightly off in another team's dynamics — maybe two of their riders had gotten into a fight the night before and weren't going to cooperate. I think my brain spun faster than my legs sometimes.

My combination of skills made me a good rider to have in the Grand Tours, where a team survived on savvy as much as on conditioning. When I finished ninth in the Tour of Spain that spring (the race now takes place in the fall), ONCE's team director guaranteed me a spot on the Tour de France roster.

I couldn't wait to tell my father. As corny as it sounds, he'd always been my biggest fan — and not because he didn't have competition. In Belgium, when a kid starts to win races, he gets adopted by locals, who form a kind of fan club. Mostly it's an excuse for the neighborhood guys to get together and drink beer at the pub before clambering onto a bus to stand beside the racecourse and scream your name. It's not so much that you're a star, but that the guys need an excuse to socialize. Still, mix beer and bike racing and a bunch of guys in Belgium and the loyalties can get pretty intense.

Even so, my father had always been, easily, my most ardent supporter. He didn't care when, at eight or nine, I turned out to be horrible at soccer, which was roughly akin to not being able to hit a ball out of the infield in America. My dad simply kept introducing me to different sports. I was terrible at every sport with a ball — except Ping-Pong, which didn't exactly herald the life I dreamed of.

I'd always ridden my bike, of course — almost every kid in Europe does, early and often. And it's not just for sport. We ride to school, to the market, into town on weekends, across town with our friends. Informal races develop—from street to street, then to the top of the biggest hill. Eventually, you're out one day and you see a big, tight group of cyclists fly by—the air from the moving pack pulling at your hair. The sound is like a locomotive. Men are shouting at each other and laughing. They're wearing bright clothes and spinning their legs impossibly fast. It seems more than anything else like a grand adventure, a bunch of grownups playing out beyond the boundaries of the schoolyards and practice fields that games are supposed to be limited to. You've just been passed by a local club, out for one of their regular training rides, or maybe one of the informal races they organize among themselves—maybe even their club championship.

My father belonged to one of those clubs; the talent and fitness levels he and his friends were able to maintain in between their obligations to their careers and families were, naturally, far below the pro ranks. But they were also much more skilled and much faster than the average riders. They raced, hard and often, and at speeds that would frighten a typical weekend warrior; they were as serious about the sport as one could get while still holding down a full-time job. I began tagging along with my dad, and the first emotion I can remember from those times is a feeling of being at ease. I just felt as if I belonged in that pack. By the time I was thirteen, I was regularly beating the adults when we'd have sprints to the finish of our training rides, or up the hills around our house. I was a natural: my heart rate stayed lower than others' as we streamed along in a tight, fast pack, and when we rose out of our saddles to sprint, it seemed as if I could spin my legs faster, or push one gear harder, or pedal with my heart jackhammering near its maximum for twice as long as the others. I also had a fluidity on the bike, not only in the motions of my legs and the way I sat, but in how I was able to navigate my handlebar through the bunch, or how I leaned into corners, or swooped around ruts, how I found holes to shoot my front wheel through when it seemed other riders were blocked. That I had some kind of gift for cycling was apparent. What none of us knew was how much of a gift. Was I going to be better than average or was I going to be pro level? And if I was pro level, was I going to be an average pro or something else?

All we knew was that suddenly I was riding faster and farther and harder than my father's friends, and he loved that. He laughed as I attacked out of the groups, and he patted me on the back at the finish of tough rides. I could hear him shouting encouragement from behind as I hammered away at the front of a group, splitting it apart. My father also knew how to encourage me in just the right way when I didn't do well. In the first real race I competed in—the first one with an official number and an entry fee—I crashed badly; my father said, simply, "Nerves," making my failure seem not like some insurmountable disaster but a mistake—an error I'd be able to easily overcome.

Belgium is known, most famously, for its gritty, hard road races in damp, chilly conditions on cobbled streets, and for long, muddy courses that are as much tests of the soul as the body; those are the races that make national heroes out of my countrymen. Cyclists from other countries believe that we Belgians are born to the rain and mud, that it is our birthright to excel when a race is at its worst. A Belgian who wins a mucky race in his home country is held up as a symbol of the nation's character. So it was sort of funny that, as my father exposed me to different kinds of racing, I turned out to be best suited to track racing. This is a very specialized type of racing that happens on a velodrome, an oval course, usually 333 meters around, that's made of smooth concrete or wooden planks. The turns are steeply banked—picture an elongated toilet bowl—so you can pedal to the top of the track then dive down into the turns to hit speeds of 45 mph or more. The bikes have one speed, can't coast—if the rear wheel is turning, the pedals are, too—and have no brakes. The frames are very short lengthwise, and the angles between the tubes and the handlebar and seat are steep, so the bike steers incredibly fast, can be whipped here and there at what feels like the speed of thought. Because of the velodrome's smooth surface, the frames can also be made extremely stiff (a regular bike generally sacrifices some stiffness for the sake of absorbing bumps and vibration from the road), which means that less of your leg power is lost through flex; when you sprint on a track bike, it's like setting off a cannon. It wasn't so much the chance to deliver power to the pedals that made me a good track racer—exposed to greater competition, I was discovering that, as it turned out, I was not going to be one of the elite of the elite in terms of physical ability—but the nature of the racing itself. Because the bikes respond so quickly to input, and because there are no brakes to get in the way of the pack's movement, track racing rewards snap decisions. I had a knack for divining which of my opponents was going to make a jump from the back of a pack, then finding my way to the outside of the pack so I could latch onto his wheel as he passed and sit behind him safe in the draft until the finish line drew near. I found that I could, better than most of my opponents, keep track of complicated events such as points races, in which points are awarded to riders throughout the race on designated laps; I always somehow knew which riders had scored each lap, and what their totals were, and how many places ahead of them I had to be on the next points lap to end up in the lead.

I was not a champion of the mud, but I was a champion.

From the time I was thirteen until it was time for me to enter the advanced education program that, in Belgium, is somewhere between a junior college and a four-year university in the U.S., I'd put together a respectable amateur career: some national championships in track events, a few race wins that anyone in Belgium would have known by name, and even, now and then, some attention from European teams looking to recruit. But my father helped keep my feet on the ground, helped me understand that beating someone my age in our home country was a lot different than, say, riding side by side with the Tour de France legends we watched together on TV.

A lot of good amateur racers put together the kind of win list I had—then settled down and became businessmen, used the connections they'd made with sponsors to get jobs in accounting firms, in marketing, running divisions of industries. The plan my father and I mapped out was that I would keep track racing while I studied for an advanced marketing degree. I thought I was probably good enough to turn pro, but I could also tell that I would never be a top pro. At every big race I participated in, there were usually two or three people faster than me. Multiply those two or three by all the races taking place in Europe in one weekend, and that put me pretty far down the talent list. And, anyway, I was almost as interested in the study of marketing. I liked being able to use my brain to do more than keep track of points.

That plan worked pretty well until my last year. Unfortunately, one of the professors at school, for some reason, resented my success outside the classroom. He found out that I'd once snuck out of a seminar two hours early so I could prepare for a race, and he used that incident to call me before a board that was in charge of academics and discipline. I still don't understand why, but the board ruled that, based on that one infraction, I wasn't going to be allowed to take my final exams. I would have to spend the summer retaking the semester's classes and then do the exams in September. There went my summer of racing. It looked like the decision I'd long put off—bike racing or marketing—had been made for me.

I went to my dad and told him what had happened. My father was a successful jewelry businessman and watchmaker, a guy who didn't take many risks.

"What do you want to do, Johan?" he asked.

I swallowed. I wanted to do everything. I wanted to do it all. I wanted to race bikes, and I wanted the kind of solid career and family my father had built for our family.

After a long pause, he said, "Johan. What is in your heart?"

"I don't want to redo my schooling," I said. "I want to try to be a bike racer now."

"Okay," said my father, the non-risk-taker. "Follow your heart. Pedal."

That season I finished second in the Tour of Belgium, which always received a lot of publicity and media coverage in our country, and I won the national time-trial championship. I would get to wear my country's colors every time I did a time trial through the whole next season. I was, in a tiny way—national compared to worldwide—a bit of a star. My potential for attracting media coverage the next season got the attention of the director of a new, small road-racing team sponsored by a bank in Liège. He offered me a contract for about seven hundred dollars a month, and I took it. We mostly did local races, and rarely went outside of Belgium. They were not glamorous, nor all that fun for spectators. Even so, my father attended as many as he could, and at the end of each one he'd seen, the watchmaker would carefully help me pull apart the tiny pieces of the race and examine them.

My career ticked along from then on as predictably as one of my father's repairs. In my second year I won a stage at a race called the Tour de l'Avenir, which doesn't mean much to Americans raised on a steady diet of the Tour de France, but which is well known in Europe. The next year I won two stages in the Tour of Switzerland and got an offer to join Lotto, one of the biggest teams in the world, and then a few seasons later moved to ONCE. My father was giddy, like a kid, not exactly happier than I'd ever seen him, but happy in a way I'd never seen in him.

He'd always loved to hang out with me and the teams I'd been on. Though he didn't always speak the dominant languages the coaches and directors used, he somehow always formed a bond with my team directors, who seemed both amused by and extremely fond of my one-man fan club. Now, at age fifty-three, when he found out I would be riding with ONCE in the Tour de France, I saw that same kind of elation in his face. I had a month and a half to prepare for the Tour, and I planned to spend some of it joining my father on his club rides.

One evening, just five weeks before the Tour, my father closed up his shop and slipped out for a late ride with his club. They weren't racers, but they were one of the strongest recreational clubs in the region, and my father was one of the strongest riders in the club—and the most well liked. My father was a major figure in town. Everyone loved him. No matter what my successes, in town I had always been my father's son. Now, proudly, he'd become the father of Johan Bruyneel.

On that ride, less than half a mile from home, he had a heart attack and died.

My world stopped.

It's hard to describe, but from the moment my younger sister, Daisy, called and said, "Dad had an accident — he's dead," my world simply stopped moving. I did the things you have to do — I drove home and comforted my mother and acted strong while coming apart inside. But the hardest, most confusing and terrifying feeling was that time seemed to no longer be really passing, as if the world were no longer really spinning, as if I had to wade through the thickness of time itself, marshaling an exhausting output of energy just to carry out the tiniest, easiest motions.

Ride? I could barely manage to move. But two days after the funeral, I got back on my bike. I knew I had to. The Tour was coming. And I owed my biggest fan a ride.

But I couldn't . . . I couldn't move my bike. I'd always trained alone when I needed to train hardest, because I could suffer more on my own. But now, I couldn't pedal hard enough or fast enough to hurt. When I would go out to ride, I couldn't will myself to really train. It was as if I were pedaling into some invisible, fluid but somehow immobile, force. I spent more time sitting in my apartment than sitting on my bike. I would look at my legs and wonder what was happening. My chest felt empty — yet heavy. Finally, one day, I set my bike deliberately against the wall of my apartment. I knew what I was doing. I was putting my bike away — and my chance to ride the Tour.

Two weeks passed.

There was now no way I could do the Tour de France; too much fitness had drained away, too much time off the bike had dulled me.

I cried one night, alone.

I cried for my father. And I cried because the Tour de France was flying away from me like one of those riders I'd never be bet-

Miles whipped past. With the wind at our backs, we were shooting our bikes forward at speeds high above 30 mph. Announcers began to mention that this could set the record for the fastest stage in Tour de France history. I didn't care.

I didn't care. For one thing, as fast as we were going, the pack was going faster. They were gulping down chunks of time with every mile. I also knew that, as fast as this group was, I had to find some way to escape off the front. Traditional cycling strategy dictated that we'd all work together to stave off the pack until the final mile or so, where we'd start attacking each other and still be able to hold off the pack with a few minutes of maximum effort. But I knew that if the race came down to those final moments, I couldn't sprint with these guys. I couldn't win in the final mile. I had to win now.

With twelve miles to go, we rode into a small, sharp hill and I stood up, poured everything into the pedals — my grief, and my anger, and my love, and my loneliness, and my regret, and my memories, and my joy, and my respect. I shot forward — five feet, ten feet — and a few riders clung to me, then gave up.

From their point of view, they were doing the smart thing; I had gone too early, I had gone alone, and I was sure to burn myself out trying to solo all that distance to the finish. But I knew something they didn't.

I'm gone, I thought. *They'll never see me again.*

I was wrong. They did see me — but they never quite caught me.

From a purely physical standpoint, I believe that what I did that day was impossible. No one could have stayed ahead of the pack with that tailwind. Here's how it works: The pack can sacrifice riders. Someone will go to the front and ride 40 mph — a ridiculous speed, a speed no one can maintain for long, a speed that explodes you after a short time and leaves you limping toward the finish line. But as soon as that rider explodes, another comes forward to keep the speed at 40 until he explodes. Then another comes up. Behind them, the leaders sit sheltered from the wind, saving their legs for the final rush to the line.

So a poor, lone rider out front, killing himself to average, say,

30 mph—a heroic speed—is still traveling 10 mph slower than the pack. And never gets to rest. It's a vicious, unforgiving sport.

I rode. I just rode. I felt no pain. I felt nothing. It was the purest experience of my life, my legs spinning, my lungs pumping air in and out of my body, my heart beating, beating, and me, my brain, the head that had worked so hard to figure out how to get me to this spot, refusing to panic or second-guess or calculate. I rode, impossibly fast and without thought.

Behind me, the pack caught the breakaway.

"There's just one rider ahead," screamed a TV announcer. "The remnant of the breakaway, just thirty seconds ahead and sure to be caught!"

I rode, in the center of the two-lane strip, right along the broken white lines, a motorcycle just behind me shooting video. The road twisted and the sun came behind me, casting my shadow forward like a rider I could chase. I chased myself. I passed under the 1-kilometer banner, people hanging over the barricades, shouting, waving their arms, and I rode, and I looked back: a wall of riders. An onrushing, crushing wall of the world's best bicycle riders with me in their sights, stripping off their sacrificial chasers at 40 mph.

I snapped my head forward and took two pedal strokes and looked back again and they were closer.

I rode. It's odd, but I just rode. I didn't summon any superhuman effort, because I'd already been at that level for the last twelve miles. I just rode, my elbows loose, my position perfect, no sign of the exhaustion that must have been tearing apart my body. It was simple: I rode in a state of grace.

The race official's car behind me flashed its lights once, twice, and I looked back, then looked down at the pavement passing beneath me for four pedal strokes, and I sat up and with the pack closing in on me like a bullet, I raised my arms to my sides as if I'd drowned. My fists were clenched. Then: into the air, into a V, the victory salute, my hands open, palms out, thirteen absolutely impossible seconds in front of the peloton.

Mario Cipollini, one of the greatest sprinters in history, won the field sprint and took second. When he crossed the line, he raised his arms in celebration, a curious move for such a proud racer. Later that season, we found ourselves riding beside each other, and Mario said, "You remember that stage you won when I raised my arms?"

"Yes," I said. I sure did.

"I thought I won," he said. "At the moment I raised my arms I saw you standing beyond the finish, straddling your bike, and I thought, 'How the hell can that guy be there? It's not possible that anyone stayed in front.'"

A lot of times, those thirty minutes just come back to me. The purity. The idea that we can exceed ourselves. That stage ended up being what was at the time the fastest day in Tour de France history — 30.7 mph. Won by me, a guy who was not a great champion but believed — and who made the most of that belief, on one magic day, by backing it up with an obsessive attention to details most would consider unimportant. It would be years before I could clearly comprehend what I'd done that day — how, in my desperation to honor my father I had, for the first time, hooked my heart and my head together and, in the alchemy of that combination, created something more powerful than the parts.

I would rediscover that lesson later, when I met Lance and we started working together. But, really, I should have figured it out long ago, because the proof of what I'd done was always there for me to see. For that stage there happened to be a special panel of legendary riders, including my homeland's icon, Eddy Merckx, the greatest all-around bike racer who ever lived. The panel was supposed to pick that day's racer who epitomized cycling grace and style. The trophy was a magnificent modern-art sculpture of a racer. I won it, but that trophy sits neither on my shelf, nor in a bar with a fan club. I had it weatherproofed, and mounted on my father's headstone with a simple inscription: THIS ONE WAS FOR YOU.

2

It Starts with Belief

I didn't need to see the figures tracking his speed or calculating his watt output or any of the other important training markers. I'd seen something more important: belief.

WHEN YOU CONSIDER how big an impact we've had on each other's lives, and on the history of cycling, it's odd that I can't really remember much about the first time I saw Lance—what he looked like or how I felt that day or anything—except for what I thought: *No brains.*

I still sometimes tease him about that, because he eventually turned into one of the smartest thinkers in the pack.

It was 1992, and Lance had just turned pro after the Olympics. Everybody in the pack in Europe had heard all about him, and there was a lot of media attention about this powerhouse from America who was going to come over and crush us. There was a lot of talk about his heart rate and his VO2 max and lots of other physical parameters. A lot of stories said his physical makeup was one in a million. In terms of my career, I was more like one of the millions: I'd won some stages and notched some impressive victories but it was clear that my time to be a superstar had passed. I was a solid worker. I was the guy who helps the guy win.

All of us in the European peloton were curious to get a glimpse of this phenomenon, and it came at a race called the Clásica San Sebastián. His first pro race ever.

He finished last.

Now, San Sebastián is a tough way to debut. The rough, jarring, broken roads weave up and down the seaside. There's no place to hide from the wind or the unpredictable, ocean-driven weather. That day, we pedaled into cold, driving rain that chilled us to our cores. It was pro bike racing at its ugliest and most blue-collar incarnation, a far cry from the sun-drenched images you see on TV, of colorful packs spinning alongside fields of sunflowers.

I knew that you couldn't judge anyone on a single day's performance in that kind of weather, especially someone who had almost no experience in conditions like that. But even so, it was kind of funny considering all the buildup and hype. The kid had power to spare — you could practically feel it emanating off him. But I could see that he also had no idea how to race in the pack, where to position himself or how to use other guys to accomplish what he wanted, how to read the race . . . none of that. So I thought: *No brains. All brawn. Not the right combo.*

The week after San Sebastián, we ended up in another race together, a five-stage race in Spain called the Tour of Galicia. There were some tough climbs in the mountainous region — ascents that could be as hard as anything I'd faced in the Tour de France. A lot of the sport's top names were there. And the kid won a stage. He won big, in an impressive way, rocketing away from thirty or forty other guys in a huge, bunched-up pack finish. He must have been going close to 40 mph when he crossed the line, even after all that climbing.

That opened my eyes. Not many new pro racers won any kind of race in their first week. And, though sprints like that can't be won without power — speeds approach 45 mph and bikes are bumping and banging off each other like dice — you also have to possess at least an innate kind of savvy, a primitive and savage instinct, to not be simply eaten alive.

We weren't friends yet — we were not even really acquaintances.

But, in the way I had of assessing all the riders around me, tracking how they rode, cataloging their habits so that I might be able to one day use that information to help me in a race, I noted the young American's exceptional strength. I remember thinking that the limits of the kid's career would be set by how much he could evolve that instinct, on his ability to intellectually grow into a chess master.

Four years later, when Lance announced that he had cancer, I felt sick to my stomach—and that was before we'd heard the worst of the diagnosis. At first, the news we gleaned from the press conference he held, and from his teammates over in Europe, seemed to be that he'd contracted testicular cancer, had the tumors removed, and was recovering. Then other news began trickling out: He had cancer in his lungs, too. In his brain. He had a fifty-fifty chance of surviving. Then 20 percent.

I still didn't know him all that well at that point. We chatted whenever we found ourselves together at a start line or in the pack. Whenever we talked, there was a natural, instant rapport. I didn't know then what he'd tell me later—that he'd grown to respect how hard I worked at winning the few stages and races I managed to, and how much thought I put into racing, how much I knew about each racer.

For my part, I'd always found his brash, aggressive style entertaining rather than off-putting. I understood that hunger for winning. I knew the kid had what it took to be a great champion. I still didn't know if he ever would be one. So when I heard the news, I felt as if I'd been punched, or as if I'd gone down in one of those senseless crashes caused by some bobble far ahead in the pack, and taken a handlebar in the gut. What a shame, I thought. What a waste. What a sad, cruel waste of all that promise.

Over the years since I'd first seen him, Lance had not developed into the chess master I thought he needed to be. But he'd kept flashing signs of that maddeningly promising instinct. He'd become the youngest rider to win the world championship road race in 1993, had won two stages of the Tour de France (even though he had never completed the race), a national championship, and a million-dollar prize for winning a series of three races in America, which everyone buzzed about for a while. For a lot of racers, that list of *palmarès*, or significant wins, would have added up to a respectable career.

But Lance had so much left he could do, I remember thinking when I heard about the cancer. If only he knew.

When I heard he'd not only beat the disease but was going to try to make a comeback, in 1998, just two years after the diagnosis, I was flabbergasted. I knew he'd undergone several operations and intense chemotherapy. Other American riders—his friends such as Kevin Livingston and George Hincapie—had told us about the brain surgery, the staples in his head, the patches of his skin scorched from the inside out by the chemotherapy chemicals.

I'd seen Lance standing among the racers at some of the early spring races in 1997. He'd come over to watch. He was bald. His eyes were sunken. And, though it's cruel to say, and I felt bad even as I knew I was thinking it, in my mind I posed what felt like horrid, rhetorical questions: A comeback? At this level of the sport? So soon?

I wished it for him. But, I wondered, if the cancer had taken away that superhuman physical power, what would the kid have left?

By 1998, my career was winding down as Lance was starting a whole new life. He had some top tens, rode a disastrous race at Paris-Nice that made him temporarily call it quits, came back because he just couldn't quit like that, and ended up winning the Tour of Luxembourg. He wasn't as bullishly powerful as he'd been, but he was finding a way to ride, to race—to win.

I followed his results pretty closely, perhaps because he seemed to be starting a second life. I was suffering the nagging injuries that plague any longtime pro cyclist, and I knew I was ready for a second life, as well. Unlike Lance, I wanted my new start to take place off the bike. By the time the Tour of Spain came toward the end of that season, I'd retired and was at the race doing some commentary for the TV channel Eurosport.

Lance finished fourth in that race—an astounding, amazing, unbelievable result. Second life? It was not just possible but could be better than the first. At the end of one stage I pushed my way through the crowd of riders and media and team personnel and found Lance.

"Whew," I said, blowing out a mouthful of breath. "Some result." I grinned.

He grinned back at me.

But it was his eyes, not his smile, that caught my attention. They were burning, an intense blue flame barely contained. It was searing in there.

It was like looking in a mirror.

Lance had lost most of that legendary power. He still rode more on instinct than intellect. But now I knew what he had left, what elevated him to a champion.

He believed.

He believed in himself.

We talked for about fifteen minutes, not about anything important. Just chatting. But when we parted, I felt better than ever about my second life, even though I wasn't sure what I wanted to do. I'd been thinking about running the riders' union. And there was always TV. I'd had an idea about organizing training camps or touring companies for avid amateur cyclists. Whatever I did, I knew it would work out.

The next day, my phone rang. It was Lance. He cut right to the point—so fast that I actually didn't know what he meant.

"So," he said, "my team needs some help. We're kind of . . . we need more structure. Vision. Can I have Gorski call you?"

"Sure," I said, when I was actually not quite sure what I was agreeing to: Consultancy? Troubleshooting?

Mark Gorski was the head of the whole team, an American I'd raced against on the track early in my career. When he called the next day, he said, "So Lance says you're interested in becoming the director of our team."

I laughed. "That's news to me," I said. I instantly thought of that fire I'd seen in Lance. "But, yes. Yes, I am."

It wasn't enough for Lance to believe in himself. He'd always had that, I realized, thinking back to that sprint he'd won his first week as a pro, back to what had seemed like the unbelievable idea that he could revive his career after cancer. But now he had to believe in more than himself. He had to believe in me. And that wasn't going to be easy, because I had some pretty crazy ideas.

After I accepted the job and told Lance I wanted to focus on winning the Tour—"we might as well win"—I kept peppering our talks and e-mails with the idea. He'd agreed right away, but I wanted to make sure he knew this wasn't a dream. This was our plan for the year. This was our whole team. This was everything.

"You'll look great on the podium of the Tour de France," I wrote in one of our first e-mails, which he saved and still has, all these years later. Another time we'd gotten together to talk about the team. There were a couple good climbers, young guys like Kevin Livingston. And good workhorses, all-arounders such as George Hincapie. But, studying the roster and charting each guy's strengths and weaknesses, it became clear that this wasn't the kind of lineup that anyone would predict capable of supporting a Tour victory.

"Johan," said Lance. "I don't know. I mean, maybe we should think about which stages we can win."

I bored my eyes into his. "No," I said. "No. We go for the overall." We stared at each other for what felt like a long time but was probably, in reality, mere seconds. I could see that the doubt wasn't coming from his heart, wasn't real. "We're going to win the whole thing," I said slowly.

Lance nodded. Then he grinned and sat back from the table we'd spread all our papers on. He shook his head, but he wasn't saying no. He was saying, "I can't believe I believe this."

But we believed it.

We believed it even as our belief took us down uncharted paths. To have any chance at winning, I knew that we had to gamble our entire season on those three weeks in July.

Bike teams weren't run that way. By tradition, a team raced a full season, from early April to late October. You were also supposed to do a lot of races—sometimes as many as a hundred or more for a full squad; and these races ranged in size from what were essentially little neighborhood events around Europe, to the big one-day races known as Classics, to the full-on multiweek Grand Tours. The little races you might find yourself in for various reasons—as a favor or a sign of respect to a rider on your team who wanted to win in his hometown or state, for instance. Or maybe the president of the company sponsoring your team wanted you to do a race near his headquarters. Sometimes the reason was logistical: the race might happen to be near your team's spring-training camp, so a full pro squad would show up to what otherwise would have been nothing more than a regional event. Sometimes you'd do races because you were pretty sure you could win them; for instance, if you had what's known as a *flahute*—the human equivalent of a racehorse known as a mudder—you might specifically set your sights on a hilly but not mountainous course on rough roads early in the year, when there was a good chance for cold or rainy conditions.

Then there were the Classics, a series of springtime races in Europe that are steeped in tradition, such as Paris-Roubaix, the Tour of Flanders, Ghent-Wevelgem, Milan–San Remo; these long, fast, devastating races generally favor strength over recovery, reward the immediate application of brute force rather than the careful unfolding of a strategy over three weeks, and always seem to require a little luck even for the most robust riders. Win a Classic, and you are a part of cycling history. Win two or more, and you are revered as a god.

From Classic season you move into the season of the Grand Tours, the multiweek races across France, Italy, and Spain. There are many other stage races slotted in the schedule around these crown jewels, such as the Tour of Switzerland, Tour de Romandie, Dauphiné Libéré, and others. Some of these are raced purely for the victory itself by the sport's second-tier teams, and some of them are used as tune-ups for the big three Grand Tours.

Into this packed schedule throw the world championships, the national championship races of each country from which a rider on your squad hails, and various other events that pop up for some reason. Hitting the full season means that riders (and directors) are almost never home from March to November, and rarely in one place for more than a week at a time. You don't live out of a suitcase; you reside in one, or so it feels.

The schedule is set up like this for two reasons: First, tradition held that racing was the best way to train for racing. At the start of a season, a director would pick out the most important races for each of his riders, then work backwards to select the races that would provide the best training for those key events. For instance, if you thought one of your riders could win a hilly classic, you'd race a lot early in the season to peak quickly, then plan for a slow period of relatively small races, where the speed and pressure would be lessened, to recover afterward (maybe missing the first of the Grand Tours) and try to come back again strong late in the season for the world or national championships. This race-based training was seen as crucial to success; it was what the greatest cyclists had always done: raced themselves into shape.

Second, a full schedule and a lot of appearances helped fulfill your obligations to your team's sponsors. Companies sponsor cycling teams, of course, for the exposure and awareness it brings their brand names. Watch carefully just before the end of the next race you see: before crossing the line, the winner takes time to zip up his jersey, pull the hem down, and straighten it so the logos read clearly and sharply. When a racer crosses a finish line with hands held high, it's not only a personal celebration but an ad for the company with its name spread across his chest. It's not only the winners who get exposure—it's the riders who go on long breakaways and have a television camera crew riding alongside them for hours, or the riders who attempt daring exploits in the mountains that attract reporters. Every photo of your team racing is an ad, every mention of a victory or a caper is what's called an "impression."

You don't get impressions when you train alone, the way I wanted to.

We were going to try something unprecedented. We were going to focus our whole schedule on the Tour de France. I was going to put our guys not into the races that would gain attention for sponsors but only into those few races that would be good preparation for the Tour. The rest of our time was going to be spent at training camps, on the routes the Tour would take.

It was a radical—no, crazy—idea.

Lance and I scouted the mountains of the Tour, the Alps and Pyrenees. He'd ride up and over two, three, four of the big mountains in a day. Then do another set the next day, logging seven to nine hours on the bike day after day. Sometimes we'd take a few of the other climbers with us. Most often he would ride alone while I followed in the car.

All the other teams were out following a traditional schedule, winning races, figuring out the stars of the season, gaining fans.

The owners and upper management of our team, amazingly, went along with the idea. When I think back on everything, that's probably one of the things that most astounds me. I don't think it was so much that they had confidence in me—I was still an unproven quantity—but something I told a group of them once, very early on.

"Look," I said bluntly. "There just isn't really that much to lose by trying this. It's not as if we're gambling with some great legacy or squandering our future. There hasn't been that much accomplished here."

As assured as I sounded, it was hard to ignore the temptations of conventional wisdom. One day in the Pyrenees, Lance's voice came over the radio we used for communication: "Hey, Johan."

"Yeah?" I thought he might want some water, or a warmer vest.

"We're this far into the year already, so . . ."

"What is it, Lance?" I looked ahead, out of the windshield. He was climbing steadily, his smooth cadence betraying nothing of the tone I heard in his voice.

"Look, I'll finish training like this for this season."

"Okay."

"But next year I'm doing the Classics."

That would mean our program had failed—that we'd go back to training and scheduling our season like everyone else. I wondered if he was right, if that's what we should be doing this year. Did Lance know something I didn't? Or was he merely having one of those moments of doubt that I, too, suffered occasionally. Should I commiserate? Should I come up with a Plan B?

Had we blown it?

"This year," I said. "This year we're winning the Tour."

On a horrible day at the beginning of May, with sleet battering the windows of the tiny hotel we were staying at and the temperature hovering right at thirty-two degrees, we had a quick breakfast at 7:30 A.M., and by nine we were on the road. Lance was riding, whirling the pedals like an eggbeater to try to stay warm. I drove the car to the base of the day's first hill, then looked over at our team mechanic, Julien, who was beside me in the front seat.

"Ugly," I said.

Julien nodded. He's an ancient Belgian mechanic, almost mystical at this point, with cult status among the world's best mechanics.

"Awful," I said.

Julien nodded.

Graham Watson, the sport's greatest photographer and one of Lance's longtime friends, had heard about our project and asked if he could come shoot for a day. Unfortunately for him, this was the day he showed up. For a while Graham rode beside Lance, perching off the back of a motorcycle to get his shots. Later, Graham told me that his motorcycle driver retired after that miserable day.

Sleet hammered down. Wind shook the car from side to side. Lance ticked off the miles, his legs turning over as if he were speeding along on a sunny day. After an hour, he crossed over the top of one climb, pointed his bike down, swooped into the valley, then attacked the next rise. On the nicest days, in the most perfect weather, the climbs of the Alps and Pyrenees are unforgiving, vicious walls upon which even the hardest men of the Tour can break themselves.

Lance was soaring. In frigid, pissing conditions. Simply flying.

"Look at that," I said to Julien. To myself.

This was one of the routes the Tour would take.

"Look," I said. "Just look at that."

Something in the way his body flowed as it drove the bike upward told me that Lance was no longer interested in doing the Classics next spring. Some vague but unmistakable change was clear in the pistoning of his legs: our plan had worked. Lance rode for eight hours that day, and at the end, at the last peak, he was just as strong as he'd been on the flat road leading to the day's first climb. I didn't need to see the figures tracking his speed or calculating his watt output or any of the other important training markers. I'd seen something more important: belief.

I'd seen it in his eyes before we started training, and it had finally come to life, out there on that hard road, in the worst conditions, far from crowds and apart from public acclaim, and neither of us ever again questioned the purity of our belief.

3

Leave Some Dents

Winners often leave behind some damage.

I'VE BEEN TOLD that being a passenger in a team car I'm driving is the wildest ride in the sport. This verdict has usually been handed down by people whose body language, despite popped-wide eyes and shaking legs, clearly communicates the sense that they are gratified to be out of the car and back onto solid, stable ground. But it has also come from team mechanics, who have lots of experience being driven through packs, from reporters who have piggybacked with many other teams, and even from the ultimate grace-under-pressure risk taker himself, Lance, who rode with me a few times after he retired and, I noticed, kept one hand clenched around the armrest much of the time.

I guess if you bump a few other cars off the road on the way to winning eight Tours de France, you get a reputation.

The first thing you have to understand is that there are more things happening on the road than you can imagine. To start with, at any moment that I'm hurtling along a narrow European lane—often half the width of a modern road—I'm just one of many, many players on the scene. Say there are twenty teams in a race; each team gets two support cars. Then there are the cars of the officials, who are all over, doing everything from ceremoniously leading the race, to watching closely for infractions (such as riders illegally getting a draft by riding behind their team cars), to dropping back close to the pack for a few minutes just to be fans and get a good look at their favorite riders. There are cars of the sponsors, who honk and wave and toss goodies to the fans, all to maximize exposure (and to give the VIPs who control the purse strings an up-close, exciting look at the sport they're spending their money on). There are what's called neutral support vehicles, top-heavy with racks full of bikes of all sizes and types, and inside stuffed to capacity with wheels and spare parts and mechanics who will spring out of the door before the car has even stopped moving so they can get a rider off a broken bike and back into the race within seconds. There are media cars that swoop in close to let print reporters, radio broadcasters, Internet bloggers, and any other type of media get a look at the action. There are miscellaneous cars for friends and families of various VIPs—politicians from towns hosting the start or finish, for instance, or the winner of a local beauty pageant, or the owner of a local bank who happens to love bike racing. Finally, add in hordes of buzzing motorcycles that wing in and out of this caravan like angry wasps, carrying photographers, reporters, VIPs, and whoever else is lucky and foolhardy enough to score a ride on the back. So at any time, around 150 cars and motorcycles might be sharing those narrow lanes with a pack of 100 or more bicycle racers.

Your position in that scrum is set by how well your riders are doing in the race; if you have one of the top guys, you get one of the cherished spots closest to the pack. And during a race, if one of your riders takes off and gets a good lead, you also get to drive up close to him, being careful to stay in a set spot between the breakaway and the pack. (If the pack starts closing in, the officials order you to move out of the gap and back behind the pack so you're out of the way again.)

That hive of cars and vehicles is not all that's going on, however. Line the gutters and sidewalks of those choked narrow lanes with screaming fans, standing three or four deep, pushing forward so they can crane their heads out and see what's coming down the road. They are shaking their fists. They are thrusting cameras out into the road to snap blind shots in the hope of getting some memorable image. They are waving flags from all over the world. They are ringing cowbells. They shout "Allez allez!" "Venga venga!" "Andiamo!" "Vollebak!" Many of them — it must be said — are intoxicated from a long day of revelry. And right there — watch out! — there's a small child darting into the road to grab a jettisoned water bottle as a souvenir.

In the best of circumstances, at your most alert and focused, safely navigating that gauntlet would be intense, nerve-racking, and dependent on a little luck, right? Now, imagine the most attention-consuming, social part of your day, whether it's running a staff meeting, or getting the family out the door in the morning with all the lunches and homework in the right bags, or getting that circle of giggling girls to listen to the soccer drill you need them to do. Now imagine having to perform that task while driving a car down that road I've described: that's being a team director.

It gets harder.

To keep track of the chess match that's rocketing down the road anywhere from 25 to 60 mph, we can't rely only on our eyes. In the first place, we're rarely that close. Because there are so many cars and motorcycles in the caravan, the officials tightly control who gets the prized spots closest to the riders. Those pictures you see on television or on race videos, where I'm driving right alongside Lance or George Hincapie or Levi Leipheimer, nodding, telling them directly what our strategy should be for the next few miles — those are rare moments. When one of them makes a breakaway I savor the chance to drive up alongside the pack, passing it, and then shoot up behind or sometimes next to my rider. (We can never get in front of them, because that would allow them to gain a huge advantage by being shielded from the wind.)

Or sometimes a rider will have a minor mechanical issue, and the team car gets to pull alongside. The rider grips the door frame. A mechanic leans out the open window — precariously arched over the bike while someone inside holds his legs—then reaches down to make an adjustment to the shifters or brakes, all while we're speeding along, while the whirring spokes of the bike wheel zing just inches from his fingers.

But even the team car of the lead director is typically kept so far behind the pack that all we get is a glimpse of all those brightly colored, slightly bobbing backs.

To understand the race, I need to rely on a lot of sources of information. Most important, to me anyway, is the feedback I get from my riders. Each of them carries a two-way radio, tucked into a snug little pocket that sits on the back of their bib shorts, with an earpiece snaking up under their jerseys and taped into their ears. I'm continually asking riders how they feel, what they see, who looks strong or weak, what the mood of the pack is. When an attack goes off the front, they let me know immediately.

There's also an official race radio, over which the commissars and referees announce things such as the names of riders in a breakaway, the time splits between groups that form, or warn the directors about upcoming dangers such as tight turns, railroad tracks, or metal-grate bridges.

Somewhere on the dashboard or windshield, I will have hung what's known as the race bible, which is a detailed map of the course that shows each street, the elevation profile of the climbs, and crucial segments such as the feed zones (where riders are allowed to grab bags of food and energy drink as they ride past). And, because almost all races are televised these days, I also watch the action on a tiny satellite TV that sits on the dash.

Now, go back to that frantic, narrow lane. It's crowded with more cars than a Los Angeles freeway. The rules of the road are more suited to a demolition derby than an average roadway. It's lined with crazed fans. Motorcycles buzz past like cartoon figures in an animated movie. Fans are leaning so far into the road that their flags are brushing the windshield, obscuring your vision for long seconds at a time.

The radio crackles to life.

It's one of your riders: "There's an attack!"

Other voices chime in, four or five riders in three different languages.

Sometimes the language barriers trip other teams up. Because I'm fluent in five languages and understand many more, the avalanche of words that crashes into the radios causes me more amusement than confusion. For instance, when the Italian teams or riders—or fans—were screaming for their leaders to attack Lance—"Dai dai dai!"—I would sometimes think, "That's right —try to outclimb Lance and you'll die die die."

In the midst of an attack, I try to affect a calm that is completely out of context. "Easy boys," I might say. "Easy now. We got this."

The official race radio bleats out the numbers of the attacking riders. You flick your eyes at the TV and catch glimpses of a red jersey, of a pedaling style you might recognize. You think they're riders far down in the standings, riders who will be ten minutes behind your top guy even if they gain five or six minutes today. Lock onto the race map for one precious second. "Easy boys," you tell the team. "Let's see who's up there." Snap the wheel away from a moto (motorcycle) on the left—then watch out for that over-zealous screaming drunk fan on the right! Squeeze the left two wheels of the car into the gutter, trying to gain every inch of clearance you'll need to keep your side mirror away from the shoulders of the riders. Start popping your palm against the horn like you're working a speed bag, and mash down that gas pedal. Go!

The way I see it, a dent is worth a win.

The point of a bike race isn't to get to the finish and have all the other team directors gather around and tell you how polite and considerate you are as a driver. The point isn't to make sure my passenger—whether it's a team mechanic, or the visiting CEO of our current sponsor, or even Lance—feels safe.

The point is to win.

If I need to bump a rival's car to get to my rider, I will do it. If I need to hurt someone's feelings to preserve what's best for my team, I will not hesitate to do it. Winners often leave behind some damage. Whatever you're doing, you have to focus on the win. It's simple, but too often forgotten. It's easy for any of us to relax our standards and let our focus slip from that ultimate goal. Do you truly need to clear your e-mail inbox to finish that big project, or can you get away with just eliminating the messages with the biggest attachments, freeing up space while saving time to focus on your ultimate goal?

On my teams, we've always focused on the win. Sometimes this meant eliminating distractions. Early on, Lance would bring his laptop computer to the races. As with everything important to him, he was obsessive about checking his e-mail and tracking the progress of his rivals via Internet reports from other races. The other guys followed suit, and soon it became clear to me that the laptop was harming our focus at least as much as it was helping us stay informed.

The laptops had to go. I was nervous about telling Lance, because he spent more time on it than anyone. But when I brought it up, explained my reasons, and pointed out three or four specific instances when I thought our focus had suffered, he gave me that aw, shucks smile he sometimes gets.

Then he shrugged his shoulders and said, "You're right. I know I have to concentrate on the Tour. Let's leave the laptops at home from now on."

And that became our policy.

Lance got it. He wasn't worried about dents. He was driving toward the big goal.

Over the years, it hasn't always been easy to get all of the riders to accept the value of dents. For instance, in some races I have to tell some of the riders that they can't ride as fast as they could in time trials—the stages where racers pedal alone, against the clock. We need those riders to save their energy, so that they can be stronger in upcoming stages when we need them to go all out to protect our leader. It's tough to ask a proud professional bike racer, in his prime, to accept a lower result that day for the sake of the team later. It dents egos.

But it works. We win.

Sometimes causing dents is harder for me than anyone knows.

In 1999, my first year on the job, the pro road champion of the United States, Marty Jemison, was on our team. Having any national champion on your squad, whether it's from the United States or Luxembourg or Kazakhstan, is a boost for the team in terms of media coverage and publicity, because national champs get to wear special jerseys in the colors of their native countries. They stand out. They guarantee interest in your team, which, coldly considered, makes your sponsors happy because their funding is translating into exposure. But doing a race with a national championship jersey amid your team is also an immense honor; at the road race, for instance, Marty had lined up against just about every American holding a professional license and come out as the winner that day—for which his reward was the chance to wear a stars-and-stripes jersey at every road race he did for the next year. (There are also national championships in time trialing and on the track and for various other events.)

There was one problem. I could tell that Marty's abilities didn't complement the other guys I'd decided to put on our Tour de France team. Obviously, as a national champion he was a great rider; he just wasn't the right kind of great rider. Marty was what's known as an all-arounder. He was pretty good at climbing, pretty good at sprinting, pretty good at holding hard, fast tempos for insanely long periods of time—the kind of combination of skills that made him a threat in one-day races over lots of different terrain, like the race for the U.S. national championship. But what he gained by having a full arsenal, he lost in terms of absolute power of each weapon. For each type of skill, there was someone on the team who was better at that particular thing. I knew that, to have any chance of supporting Lance in the Tour, we needed a team assembled of the strongest possible components, rather than complete cyclists.

If I took Marty to the Tour de France, it would make our sponsor, U.S. Postal Service, very happy. But it would unbalance the team.

I couldn't sleep. My stomach churned. My head hurt. How could I leave the national champ sitting at home during the biggest bike race in the world? For days this went on. Finally, privately, I told Marty the news.

He was stung. He was hurt. And the worst thing was, I knew that in one sense he had a right to be upset—he was the national champion! Then the news leaked out that, in his first year as director, the guy running the largest American team wasn't taking the American national champion to the biggest race in the world. I got crucified. I also spent a lot of time explaining my rationale internally.

But I knew I'd done the right thing, and the proof came at the end of July, when Lance rode into Paris for his first victory in the Tour de France.

Winners dent things.

I was reminded of this—literally—some years later, in the 2005 Tour de Georgia. A twenty-seven-year-old American, Tom Danielson, had joined our team. Some were calling him Lance's heir apparent. In terms of physiology he certainly seemed destined for big things; in the lab performance tests, his numbers often rivaled or exceeded those of Lance. He was super lean, and on the steepest of roads could shoot his bike forward. But Tom, who had been a pro road racer since 2002, had never quite been able to put everything together for that first big win.

There were three other Americans on rival teams—Levi Leipheimer, Floyd Landis, and Bobby Julich—who wanted a victory badly in the six-day, 550-mile race, and they each had the talent and the teams to win. We'd brought a top squad—genuine stars and up-and-comers such as Viatcheslav Ekimov, one of the most experienced and fierce riders in the pack; Jason McCartney, a young American who impressed me with his ability to analyze and interpret a race; José Azevedo and José Rubiera, both brilliant, lean climbers; plus Lance, who had won the previous Tour de Georgia, and Danielson, our designated leader. I wanted him to win this race.

Landis became our number one rival when he leapt into the lead in the stage 3 time trial, going up by exactly a minute over Tom. Levi, ten seconds ahead of Tom, sat fifty seconds off the lead. The next day, on a course that crossed five mountains through thunderstorms and terrifying bolts of lightning, I sent Chechu —Rubiera—off to try to weaken Landis, see if he could be forced to chase so that Danielson could sweep by near the end to gain time. Landis ended up isolated from his team after the final climb, but finished strongly and, with only one more mountain stage to go the next day, hung on to his one-minute lead. The whole race was going to come down not only to one day, I thought, but to one climb: the last climb of the race, Brasstown Bald, a three-and-a-half-mile wall that rises to nearly forty-eight hundred feet. Its pitches are steeper than anything the pros ride in the Tour de France.

On race day, we kept hearing reports that there were 45-mph winds on Brasstown, and that temperatures were dropping. And I could feel the winds buffeting the car as I careered up and down the race caravan. As the pack rolled toward the peak, I heard something shocking: it was snowing up there. Okay, I thought, the harder the better. Let's turn this into a brawl.

On the climb before Brasstown, I sent Lance to the front with orders to crack the race apart. He wasn't in top shape, and he couldn't have mustered his best effort day after day—and at this stage in the season we didn't want him to—but like any great champion he could always, at any time, pull one spectacular effort from his body. He drilled into the slope, and only a few guys could hold his wheel: Tom, Levi, Floyd, and a few others. That was punch one.

Brasstown looked as if it were a tunnel that had been dug through an earth made of cycling fans—they were everywhere, standing on each others' shoulders, cheering, yelling, running alongside us. Wind rocked the car back and forth, and I could see the racers pushed sideways, from one paint stripe to the next. Snowflakes darted before us, melted on the windshield. I nosed my car past several others, crowded a moto to the side.

"Go!" I shouted to Tom.

He immediately dropped Landis, and Lance, without needing to be told to do so, dropped back and began shadowing Landis. Tom drove forward, and from out of the knotted pack came Levi, pulling himself up to Tom's wheel. The two of them powered away, up the hill.

We'd executed our strategy perfectly. Tom had dropped Landis, and would continue to gain time on him. But we were going to lose if we didn't punch again—Levi, who was right on Tom's wheel, was ten seconds ahead of him in the overall standings. All Levi had to do to win was stay within ten seconds of Tom, hang right there on his wheel to the top.

The last half mile of Brasstown is one of the cruelest stretches of road in pro racing. It is exposed and windy and cold, and the pitch is so steep most people—nonpros—literally cannot ride their bikes up it. Tom and Levi were riding side by side, eyeing each other, showing their strength so the other might wilt.

I said, calmly, so it would carry more weight at a time when a yell was expected: "Now, Tom." And it was as if I'd touched a fire to gunpowder. Tom blasted forward. Levi, who'd been alongside him, fell back behind and swung over directly behind Tom's wheel, pacing off it. "He's on your wheel," I said to Tom. "You can drop him. You're going to drop him. You will, Tom. You can drop him. Drop him. Drop him, Tommy. You can drop him."

I could start to feel that rhythm I sometimes got when I spoke into Lance's ear, that mysterious process where my voice and the rider's pedal strokes seem to mesh, to anticipate each other, to feed off each other. When I said "Drop him" again, Tom did. He rolled through the last, right-hand switchback alone, somehow got even faster, and crossed the line fourteen seconds in front of Levi, and a full 1:09 ahead of Landis.

We had bashed the field into submission. It was a brutal, unforgiving form of bike racing. The whole race had been like that —which might explain why, after one stage, I found myself face to face with one of the race officials.

"We're um . . . we're going to have to fine you for some driving violations," he said.

I didn't say anything.

"Those were, um, some pretty insane moves," the official said. He sounded almost apologetic, or maybe he was intimidated by the prospect of having to reprimand the director of a team that had, at that point, won six Tours de France in a row. "I know it's probably different in Europe, but the driving is less aggressive here. We have to fine you."

I smiled at him. I didn't want him to feel bad.

I said, "It's okay. If I don't get fined, I'm probably not doing my job."

His forehead crinkled, then he walked away.

When I got to the finish and rushed over to congratulate Tom Danielson, winner of the Tour de Georgia and victor of one of the most brutal one-two mountain attacks I'd ever been a part of, I was stepping out of a very battered, very worn-out car.

4

Do Whatever It Takes to Communicate

The true value of communication is often not so much what you say to each other but the simple, powerful fact that you care enough to say something to each other so often.

THE BIGGEST ADVANTAGE of race radios is not what you think it is.

There's no doubt that the ability to both listen and talk to my riders as they spin along the road gives me greater strategic ability than team directors used to have. I realized this literally before anyone else: we were the first team to put radios on all of our riders—during my very first year on the job, in 1999.

When I was still racing in the early and mid-1990s, only the leaders of teams had radios. I wasn't the top rider, but I had built such a reputation as being the eyes and ears of the pack that I ended up regularly being picked to broadcast my analysis back to the director. I remember thinking at the time how much more effective it would be if everyone on the squad could communicate instantly. So when I got the job running Lance's team, I started working on that right away—and I realized why no other teams had done it. Getting all those radios to consistently and clearly work turned out to be a horrendous technical challenge.

The frequencies are used by all the other communication devices needed at races, so it was tough to find bandwidth we could rely on. And the simplest logistical problems ended up being surprisingly tough to solve. For instance, all bike jerseys have pockets on the back, which seemed the logical place for riders to carry their radios. This worked fine when only the stars used radios. But once the domestiques—the riders designated to support the rest of the team—got radios, there were complications. A domestique might be asked to come back to the team car to retrieve as many as five to seven water bottles for the rest of the team. A pocket with a radio in it was a pocket we couldn't use. We ended up having our clothing sponsors custom-build pouches onto the back of our bib shorts to hold radios, a special feature that's stock today. (Some bibs even have integrated controls in the straps now.)

That first year, the radios were a huge advantage because we could react faster. But now that all the teams have them for all their riders, the field has been evened. Everything—for everyone—happens faster. For instance, we used to have to spend two minutes or more figuring out which riders had made it into a breakaway, as chatter made its way rider by rider through the pack and back to the team cars. That gave the attacking riders a lot of time to organize and put distance between themselves and the pack. Now in twenty to thirty seconds I can marshal the whole team to the front to mount a chase if we decide that the riders who got away have to be brought back to the pack.

When it comes to tactics, the radios don't suddenly make you say brilliant things; they merely let you communicate the same things more quickly. So, in terms of strategy, the benefit is not that great. People always seem surprised to hear me say that; I think fans expect me to be whispering some kind of top-secret tactical code to the riders. But after spending seven years in Lance's ear, I can tell you that you'd be disappointed, in fact, if someone handed you a transcript of everything Lance and I had ever said to each other over the radios. The content is more mundane than sparkling.

When Lance would attack, I might tell him what was happening behind: "They're dropping off. They're sliding back. Their shoulders are bobbing now. You got it. You got it."

I might announce the gaps: "You have ten feet," I'll say. "Twenty feet." Then, as he continues to pull away, I'll switch over from distance to the currency that really matters to us: "You're up by thirty seconds."

There are some light moments. When I want to give water and energy drinks to the team, I like to say, "Boys, the bar is open."

In the 1999 Tour de France, Lance was in the yellow jersey after winning the time trial. The race hadn't yet entered the mountains, where the top climbers figured they could take away the jersey by blowing up Lance—he'd never been able to ascend like a champion. When we got to the Alps, we faced an eighty-mile stage that ended with an eighteen-mile climb up a mountain called Sestriere. Sure enough, two of the race's best climbers attacked and got a gap. Ivan Gotti and Fernando Escartín were more than half a minute up the road; it wasn't so much the time difference as the fact that the climbers wanted to crack Lance—to show that he couldn't take such hard racing.

Lance sat in a trailing group. We were playing it safe. Then, with five miles left to climb, I said softly, "It's time to go."

Lance swung out of the group and accelerated.

"You gapped them," I said. He kept accelerating, and I kept announcing distance and time. In just over half a mile he leapt across more than two-thirds of the vertical wasteland between us and the leaders, Gotti and Escartín. His legs were like pinwheels, a mesmerizing spiral of color.

"Smooth," I said, "Go. Go, go go go go, smooth, easy, sit, sit, don't stand, spin spin spin. You're coming up on them. You're coming up on them." And then he was with them, right on their wheels, sitting at the front of the Tour de France in the cruel mountains with two of this year's top climbers, two of the men who figured they'd put a cap on this brash young American's improbable comeback story. Return to the sport from cancer? Yes. Win the Tour de France against the likes of us? No way.

Lance looked loose, relaxed. I said, "Give me some more," and he accelerated. Gotti and Escartín couldn't follow. "More," I said, and then began ticking off the gap he'd created between his back wheel and their front wheels: "Two bike lengths, three, four . . ."

I'd known for months, of course, that Lance could ride like this. It was what we'd trained for. It was no surprise — except that there it was, really happening, on the road of the Tour de France, on the last, toughest climb of the mountains that were supposed to be his weakness.

I began speaking a stream of encouragement into Lance's ear: "Go, go, go, come on, Lance, pedal, pedal, pedal, that's it, Lance, smooth, now, now now now, yes yes yes." It was the rhythm that came to me first, not the words. The true value of communication is often not so much what you say to each other but the simple, powerful fact that you care enough to say something to each other so often. It's the connection that matters. Hearing each other. Speaking to each other.

At some point, as he neared the finish line, and what would be, so far, the greatest triumph of his cycling career, Lance's voice crackled through the radio: "Johan, do you like apples?"

I looked over at Thom Weisel, the owner of the team, who was riding in the passenger seat beside me that day. I raised my eyebrows. Had Lance cracked? Was he babbling?

"Um, yes," I answered hesitantly. "We like apples, Lance." I paused. "Why?"

"Then how," he said, "do you like them apples?"

And he crossed the finish line, hands high, head tipped to the clouds.

Everyone loves that story — including me. But when it comes to getting my voice inside Lance's head, I often think of a private moment the two of us shared, one that shows it's really not about radios or even words, but about communicating.

Proclaiming my belief that he could win the Tour de France wasn't the only radical statement I made to Lance when we decided to work together. I also told him he had to change his whole style of pedaling—that he had to, in effect, break the mold of everything he knew about propelling a bike. This wasn't going to be easy. Even on a casual ride, a cyclist makes about eighty to ninety pedal strokes a minute. To use a round number for ease, that's somewhere around five thousand revolutions every hour. Pros ride four or five hours a day, so figure twenty-five thousand pedal strokes a day. You can bet they ride two hundred days a year, easy, which puts them at around 5 million pedal strokes each year. Lance had been training and racing since he was fifteen. That meant that, by the winter of 1999, his body had learned to pedal a certain way by repeating the motion about 65 million times.

I had a few months to undo that.

I believed that, just as he had often in the past used his raw horsepower to compensate for his lack of experience, he'd relied too much on sheer power in the mountains. If he could learn to spin the pedals faster, he'd be able to take advantage of his superhuman aerobic capacity and genetic physical ability—he could ride aerobically while others suffered and gasped for breath. He'd be able to save those power surges and unleash them in full at key moments, rather than gradually expend that energy.

To accomplish this, Lance had to retrain his body to spin the pedals at 100–120 rpm while staying seated. His instinct, at this point, was to rise out of the saddle and stomp a hill into submission. All during that long winter and spring, as he rode Europe's mountains, climb after climb after climb, hour after hour, day after day, I'd follow behind and, when he rose out of the saddle, whisper through the radio that he had to sit back down and spin.

I could see him suffering. I knew that standing up to pedal must have felt good—natural, strong. "Sit," I'd say into the radio, knowing that my hated command was echoing in his ear. "Spin. High cadence, Lance. High cadence."

He'd sit, and spin his legs faster, and even though sometimes his heart rate would go up, he was sparing his muscles. His body was becoming more efficient. It was working.

"Sit," I said, over and over, almost like a chant.

It wore on both of us. We each, over the course of that training, grew weary of the routine. I wanted to stop telling him to sit. He wanted to stop hearing it. But we kept it up. We had to. We had to make seated, high-cadence pedaling feel right. One day, Lance couldn't bring himself to listen to me anymore. As he settled into yet another climb, he ripped the earpiece away from his head and rode on. I could see the cord swaying free, arcing like a pendulum with the motion of his legs.

The road steepened and Lance rose out of the saddle. Out of habit, I started to speak into the radio.

He was out of the saddle, attacking the pedals. I laid my palm against the car's horn. Brrrrrraaaaaaaa! Brrraaa! BRAAAAAAAAA!

Lance sat back down, then looked over his shoulder. He spun those pedals, around and around.

He rose again, and I blared the horn at him.

He sat. He'd heard me. More important: he'd listened.

The future seven Tour de France champion spun the pedals as fast as he could.

5

To Earn Confidence, Confide

*You have to be open to those moments when you
should extend, and invite, confidences large or small.*

WHEN I RODE the 1995 Tour de France, I was having a good
run of luck. I'd won a stage early on, and my team had not
one but two of our top riders contending for the yellow jersey—we had a chance to dethrone the mighty Miguel Indurain,
who had won four Tours in a row and had been widely expected to
dominate in this one, his fifth.

There was no mistaking the fact that Indurain rode on a plane
far above most of us. He crushed the field every time there was
a time trial—the solo race against the clock. And when the Tour
had entered the Alps, he'd climbed strong and smooth, using his
amazing horsepower to drive his big body up the roads; amid the
fluttering, darting motions of the tiny climbers, Indurain looked
like a bear loping up a hill amid a swarm of bees. There was a serenity to his riding that was unsettling to the rest of us, suffering
along just to stay near him.

But on a climbing stage to the town of Mende, my teammate
Laurent Jalabert made a gutsy, early attack, riding away from the
pack to gain so much time that he just missed taking over the yellow jersey. (His ride that day was deemed so heroic that the climb
was renamed in his honor as the Montée Laurent Jalabert.)

Suddenly, Indurain seemed vulnerable. After four years of domination, the pack had a race on its hands. It seemed that if someone could surprise Indurain and take time away from him in unexpected places, a new champion might be crowned. Jalabert was also contending for the green jersey. The green jersey is one of the races within the race that makes the Tour de France such a complex and entertaining competition — there are so many ways to win.

There is the overall standing, of course, which is called the general classification (GC) and is figured out by adding each rider's total accumulated time over the entire race. The GC leader gets to wear the yellow jersey. Then each day, someone can win a stage and get to stand atop the podium for that. The green jersey, known as the points jersey or the sprinter's jersey, is awarded to the rider who accumulates the most points by being the first to cross certain spots along the course and at the finish lines. A polka dot jersey, known as the King of the Mountains jersey, is awarded to the rider who crosses the most mountaintops in the lead. There's also a white jersey, given each day to the highest-placed GC rider under the age of twenty-five. Also at the end of each stage, a special panel votes on the day's most aggressive rider, who then gets to wear a black-and-red number the next day (instead of the traditional black-and-white). A team competition is decided by adding the accumulated time of all the members of the squad. Finally, there's even an unofficial but compelling race for something called the *lanterne rouge,* an honorific that goes to the last-place rider; it's an odd but very real honor to be the final racer in the overall standings — it means you were too tough to quit.

Though Jalabert had launched the attack that exposed Indurain's vulnerability, we all thought that it was our teammate Alex Zülle, who would win a stage in the race that year as well, who had the best chance of anyone at slipping onto the top step of the podium should Indurain crack. Zülle, a powerful, stoic, and bulldoggish Swiss rider whose career would span mine and extend well into Lance's, was a former world time-trial champion, and a great all-arounder who in the course of his fourteen years of competition would win two Tours of Spain, three stages of the Tour of Italy (and two of the Tour de France), and the Tour de Suisse. He was a gifted, phenomenal bike racer who had the bad luck of having his career parallel that of both five-time winner Indurain and seven-time winner Lance. It was no wonder we all believed he could win that day in 1995. As my team's rolling lieutenant, I had my eyes, ears, legs, and brain working overtime; I felt as if I had to keep track of every move and every rider to give Zülle a shot at the greatest achievement in sport.

Then, in one instant, all of that seemed beside the point.

The race had just entered the Pyrenees, and we'd climbed up and over a mountain called the Col de Portet d'Aspet. In the context of the Tour de France it's nearly a gentle climb — around eleven miles up to a height just over three thousand feet, with a nice, steady grade that lets you mostly sit and grind it out. The peloton climbed up and over and started down, stringing out into little packs and long, long lines of single riders.

On descents, a pro pack tends to go from its arrowhead, wedge-like shape to a string. The safest and quickest line — the path you want to take through the turns — is to swing wide before a turn, ride sharply across the inside, then exit wide again. Taking that line when riders are spread three or more abreast across the road can be difficult, so the racers tend to order themselves more or less directly behind each other. Also, much of the passing happens in corners, so you want to leave plenty of room on the road to maneuver past other riders.

Because so many riders are lined up, when one of them skids, gets a flat, or fails to make it around a corner (occasionally someone goes so fast they can't make a turn, and flies straight off the road), a chain reaction begins and a whole mess of cyclists crash.

There was a big wreck as we were coming down the Aspet — as usual, none of us knew what had caused it, but we saw fifteen or twenty riders off their bikes, a lot of guys lying on the ground, some of them standing up and holding their elbows or arms, a few lifting their bikes off the ground, making sure their wheels would still spin without hitting the frame. A squad of medics surrounded at least one of the riders. It's an unnerving scene, but not that unusual in the Tour.

Those of us who had been lucky enough to stay upright continued down the climb and rode on toward the finish. After a while, the news began to trickle into the pack, at first via the few riders who had race radios, then person to person: Fabio Casartelli had died in the crash.

Casartelli was a young, affable Italian, someone who innately understood how to conduct himself professionally and perform at the top level of the sport without becoming a big ball of stress. His manner was loose but not goofy. I think the word most frequently used to describe him was "friendly."

He was also a fierce competitor. Among other top prizes, he'd won the gold medal at the 1992 Olympic road race (beating, among other highly favored competitors, another powerhouse kid by the name of Lance Armstrong). I knew that Casartelli had ended up on Motorola, the same team as Lance, and that he had a beautiful wife and month-old baby at home.

We were crushed. All of us. The mood at the end of the stage was somber, dark, muted. Over the course of the month-long Tour de France, it's inevitable that there are crashes—so many that sometimes by the end of the race you can't remember them all. Bikes break. Bones bust. Hopes are smashed and, sometimes, dreams, too. Through it all, every one of us is aware not only of the risk inherent in the way we've chosen to live our lives, but of the fact that the risk is serious enough to cost us those lives. We know death is a possibility every race; we just never expect it to happen—maybe because, through a combination of skill and timing, almost every one of us has escaped that fate by a lucky break as thin as a hair. Guys hit cars and live, smash through windshields, sometimes careen into spectators, run over cats and dogs, collide during sprints, and slip on gravel or wet roads or dropped water bottles, or hit curbs, or touch tires ... really, the list of ways to crash is endless. And so, it seems, is our ability to escape alive.

But it only seems that way. Casartelli reminded us that we were nothing more than lucky. He'd fallen and slid across the road, and by chance ran into the curb, fracturing his neck and skull.

The news rippled through the pack that Motorola was thinking of abandoning the race, of not showing up the next day. I heard that Lance, in particular, had been stricken with grief and wanted to fly home to be with his mother and friends. As all the racers gathered that night in the hotel dining rooms to eat dinner, then went off to get massages, to relax, to catch up on news or sleep, word spread that Casartelli's wife had met with his team and asked them to ride in his memory.

The next morning, the entire pack assembled in rows behind Motorola, whose riders were spread out under the start banner the width of the road. There was to be no race; only a rolling memorial, the Tour de France's own kind of funeral procession. Just behind the Motorola riders was their team car. For eight hours it drove in front of the pack, and as we pedaled softly and quietly over the roads of France I would look up from time to time, up to the rack atop the team car, where instead of a full complement of backup bikes there was just one: Casartelli's blue bike, draped with black ribbon.

Gears clicked and wheels spun, wind whispered. For eight hours we thought of Casartelli, and our own close calls. We quietly spoke of others who had died, those we'd raced with back home as kids, famous legends we knew only through stories, racers in far-off lands we knew only through their fates. Of course I thought of my father. Of the stage I'd won for him.

At the end of the day, the entire Motorola team crossed the finish line at once. As I crossed the line, in that pack of mourners, I told myself that, as hard as it would be, I had to make the line I'd just ridden over truly be the finish of that day. I had to stop thinking of Casartelli, death, danger. The race demanded it. Jalabert and Zülle deserved my best. Indurain—the great champion— deserved to be challenged by the best. Casartelli's wife had wanted his team to ride on, and Casartelli himself would have wanted no more funeral processions—like any top pro, he would have wanted us to race as hard as we could, all the way to Paris.

And the race was back on. The next day I found myself countering attacks, analyzing breakaways, calculating time differences, and doing all I could to help my team protect Zülle as he stalked Indurain. When we rode into Bordeaux at the end of the day there was almost a palpable sense of relief emanating from the pack: this excruciating, challenging, exhausting racing—this was something we knew how to do.

The following day I was covering breakaways again when I ended up in a leading group of twenty-five that built a good gap on the pack. Lance was in there. We nodded at each other, exchanged greetings, but he seemed preoccupied, and I figured he was still mentally beat by Casartelli's death. The group chugged along, going just fast enough to stay away from the pack, but not so quickly that we would start to crack each other apart and disintegrate. I was marking time, watching everyone for clues to our next move. And studying Lance.

The kid had still never yet finished a Tour de France. People said the mountains always beat him, but I thought that he was the one beating himself, with the way he rode, trying to batter the earth itself with his powerful pedal strokes, as if he might stomp the world into submission. Once again, I wished I had his physical talent to go with my racing instincts.

We were rolling along like that, harder than most people could ever ride but, for us, easy enough for me to entertain such musings. Guys were adjusting the straps of their shoes, rolling their shoulders, checking the speed and heart-rate readings on their handlebar-mounted computers. But, really, we were all secretly starting to watch each other. There were about twenty-five miles to go to the finish in Limoges; that was still a long way, and certainly too early for someone to try to get away. But it was time to start setting up, finding the people you wanted to draft when it got hard, figuring out who looked weak and who looked strong, and—

Lance attacked!

It was as if he'd been launched out of a catapult.

Instantly there was fifteen feet of empty pavement between him and the front of our group. Then thirty feet. Guys looked at each other. Fingers twitched against shift levers. Then we did nothing.

He'd gone too early. Way too early. There was no way he could last out there alone for twenty-five miles. Sure, he'd delivered a punishing, terrifying show of raw power in the way he'd leapt away from us. But the kid, once again, had overestimated his ability to pummel the Tour de France into submission. We would catch him, for sure.

Then, as I watched the tiny blue figure ride off into the distance and disappear around a corner, I thought of Casartelli, the tragic mortal I'd worked so hard to put out of my mind.

And I thought of my father.

And I thought of another Tour de France stage, the one I'd won in tribute to my dad, the one in which I'd done the same thing Lance just had — ridden away from the pack way too early.

Was it possible?

I am not what anyone would traditionally call a religious man. I suppose you could say I am more what could be described as spiritual, although I never profess to have the answers to questions about our souls, about the afterlife, about the meaning of what is here and what might be out there somewhere waiting for us. All I know for sure in this area is that when I won that stage way back in 1993, my father was with me.

I'm not saying I saw him, or heard him, or that he helped me power the bike. I guess I'm not saying anything much, except that I was aware, every pedal stroke, of my father.

When Lance won the stage into Limoges that day — a full minute ahead of us, even after we started chasing as hard as we could — he punched the air in front of him, and pointed skyward, and raised his face to the clouds. The finish was a madhouse of cheering people, and weeping people — fans and racers and support staff alike — and when reporters and TV cameras and radio microphones surrounded Lance, he said, "Today I rode with the strength of two men."

· · ·

The next day, as the pack spun out of town and we began another stage, I pedaled up beside Lance and said, "Whoo, I didn't think you were going to make it."

He looked over at me and smiled, and it was genuinely happy but somehow thankful as well. He said, "I knew I was gone," and it did not sound at all like bragging.

"Yes?" I said, thinking back to how I'd felt. "I said to myself, 'What is he thinking? It's so early.'"

Lance nodded and said, "No kidding, I knew I was gone. Once I had ten meters I knew you guys couldn't catch me. I just . . . it was . . . I mean . . ."

I had an instinctual urge to tell him the things I'd experienced when I rode that day with my father. But something held me back. We were professional racers. We lived a hard life, one that depended in part on our ability to search out each other's weaknesses. I had, by now, trained myself to automatically scan the pack as I rode. Even while I might be chatting with someone beside me, I was paying attention. Had that guy's right knee been wobbling all along, or was it just happening because he was tired? I'd file that observation away and recheck it when I saw him in front of me again another time. Or maybe in the course of the idle chatter that happens when the race is humming along but not murdering us, a rider might tell me about a superstition he had, or how much he disliked traveling, or the taste of the water in some province. Because I'd been on the receiving end of so much data, I understood intimately that, as a pro, just about anything we revealed might be used against us by an opponent at some time in the future. Like Indurain, it was best to be implacable, or so the wisdom held.

"I felt the same way," I blurted. "When my father died, I won a stage for him and I attacked early—too early—but I knew I was gone."

Lance cocked his head and kind of narrowed his eyes.

I'd come this far, so I just went on ahead. I said, "I felt him with me that day."

Our eyes connected, and Lance, ever so slightly, nodded his head again.

"Anyway," I said, "great ride."

We pedaled off to tend to our separate duties to our separate teams.

I don't exactly walk around to everyone I see and share my most private moments with just anybody, just to forge intimacy. It doesn't work that way. You can't blab the secrets of your soul to everyone in earshot, or even everyone on your team. But I think you have to be open to those moments when you should extend, and invite, confidences large or small.

When I hired Dirk Demol as one of my assistant team directors, I admitted to him that one reason I wanted him for our team was that I had never been good at the one-day Classic races such as Paris-Roubaix and Flèche-Wallonne. In those races, the tactics play out more quickly, and brutality can trump ingenuity, and there are fewer chances to come back from bad luck such as a flat tire or slipping out in a corner. I had an undeniable knack for figuring out how a race would develop over three weeks, but when it came to the split-second decisions of the one-day races, I wanted someone who was better than me. That was Dirk, a Belgian like me, but one who had specialized in the elements we were supposed to: he'd won on the cobblestones of Paris-Roubaix way back in 1988. When I hired him as an assistant team director, I admitted to him why. I think my honesty allowed Dirk to operate in the Classics, and other races, without wondering what I'd think, or how I'd criticize his strategies.

I'm not a big fan of team-building games. I don't like to have everyone stand and divulge something about themselves we don't know. Instead, I try to create opportunities in which the team riders have their own chance to sense moments for confiding. For instance, on a multinational team like ours, it's difficult to avoid the formation of cliques by nationality. As much as I can, I try to split racers from the same nation between races. When two have to be at the same race—sometimes your best climbers are from Spain, for instance, and you want them at that race no matter what—I make sure they don't room together. I want the riders to mix, and learn words in each other's language, and hear each other call home, and borrow shampoo if they need to. The Americans might try to explain ZZ Top lyrics to the Europeans. Somewhere in that messy exchange of ideas and jokes and everyday actions, we end up confiding in the others. We gain confidence in our friendships.

I don't think I believe in fate, or even destiny. I think life is what we make of what we're given. Some people might be tempted to see some sort of grand plan in the fact that Lance and I both found ourselves having one of the most amazing rides of our lives in nearly identical circumstances, and that we somehow each broke through the wall of stone that isolates professional racers, and then ended up years later coming together again to win a record seven Tours de France.

Me? I think it comes down to what makes up a winner. I believe the two of us were operating on winner's instinct—not just when we rode, but when we each took the chance of exposing a sensitivity that's rare in a sport that demands you appear invincible. I think on some level, some very deep level—call it unconscious, or primal, or animal instinct or spiritual or what you will—both he and I sensed an advantage to be had by connecting in that way.

Lance and I were still not what anyone would call close friends after that one exchange; but in some important way, in that moment we were closer than many friends ever get. We always had that unusual bond, forged on those two days years apart, and I know that is part of what pulled us back together as team director and champion. We never spoke much about that day, even years later when we were the closest of friends. It was too intimate.

6

Bluff When You're Weak—
And When You're Strong

*Strength and weakness live together, inside each
of us, and we are fools if we do not see both when
we look at someone else.*

A S THE ROAD tilted upward for the first mountain stage of
the 2001 Tour de France, something astonishing happened:
the smooth, circular pedal strokes that Lance had used to
dominate his first two Tour de France wins, in 1999 and 2000, began to falter. His front wheel, nearly imperceptibly at first—but
there it was again—wobbled. The fittest, most determined bike
racer in the world began to drift backward through the pack. The
racers streaming around him now were silent, shocked, trying to
simultaneously look at Lance and not visibly stare at him—it was
like seeing your father cry for the first time or fail to lift a heavy
box. Standing up, laboring over his bike, working his arms, at the
last possible second Lance lunged onto the very back of the pack
and visibly fought for breath.

Our team had been expected to follow what had become generally recognized as our signature game plan once the race got to
the mountains: go to the front, take the lead, drive a hard pace and
drag the rest of the pack to the foot of the climb, at which point
Lance would leap upward and smash the race to bits.

It wasn't happening. Lance rolled his head. His pedal strokes looked choppy. From the radio embedded in the dash of our team car, and from the TV mounted above it, I could hear commentators going wild in English, French—flip the channels and there was the same stream of disbelief in Italian, German, every language you could imagine. The voices were screaming: Something's wrong with Armstrong! Armstrong appears weak! He falls to the back!

Just as frantically as the airwaves were shooting the news out to the public, the word was spreading among the pack: Armstrong is at the back.

Jan Ullrich, the mighty German racer who was our chief rival, the one person in the world that both Lance and I felt had a chance to beat us, marshaled his team. As one unit, they gathered at the front and hardened into a ball of speed and began to drive the pace higher and higher.

"Could Armstrong crack?!?" shouted a commentator. "Is this the end of his dominance?"

At the start of the 2001 Tour de France, I knew our team was strong all around but also that it might run into trouble. On paper we had a good squad. Besides Lance and his longtime, ultraloyal lieutenant and friend George Hincapie, there were two of the best climbers in the world, from Spain. We had Victor Hugo Peña, a Colombian mountain climber who, rare for someone from his country, could also motor on the flats. There was Eki—Viatcheslav Ekimov—an experienced, savvy Russian who could drag the entire pack along for hours if need be. I'd brought Steffan Kjaergaard, a Norwegian, specifically to help us in the team time trial (what's known as the TTT). I rounded out the squad with two of the best American climbers, including a kid named Christian Vandevelde, who, I thought, would have what it took to be right there at the end with Lance when the mountain roads became nearly unbearable. All in all, it was a team that could support Lance on the leg-melting climbs, that could eat up the long, flat, and rolling miles

that led to the important climbing stages—and that would perform well in the TTT.

I figured the TTT might play an important part in sorting the
winners from the losers that year. In the team time trial, the entire squad races against the clock; everyone on the team gets the
same time. So a strong rider who was a legitimate contender could
lose minutes if he had a weak, slow team—effectively ending his
chance to step on the podium in Paris. Conversely, by bringing a
team crafted to do well in the TTT, we might gain valuable time
on some of our key opponents, forcing them to start the mountain
stages, which began days later, with a deficit they might never overcome. I wanted our opponents to start racing against each other
for second and third, rather than thinking they had a shot at taking the lead in the mountains. So I'd deliberately assembled a team
that could perform very strongly in the TTT, even though it meant
sacrificing some of our depth when it came to climbing talent.

In the previous Tour, in 2000, Lance had not merely won but
established himself as the lion of the peloton—what's known as
the patron. The title is a little bit mayor, a little bit Don Corleone.
It's not that the race is conceded to the patron; it's just that the patron sets the tone for the race. Out of respect for and in deference
to his power, the pack generally allows the patron to decide which
stages will be hard, which will be rolling rest days, who gets into
the breakaways and gets a chance to win a stage.

But a patron's hold is fragile. At the first sign of weakness, the
reign snaps to an end and the pack becomes like a medieval country without a king.

To prevent this chaos—an unpredictable race is bad when
you're the favorite—a patron first needs a team that can take control of any stage. A patron's team must be able to go to the front
and keep the pace high for mile after mile when necessary, going so
fast for so long that nobody has the heart to try to attack and break
away. A patron's team must also be able to chase down any break
it deems a threat to its leader, or coerce the pack into not chasing a breakaway that poses no such threat: if someone fifty minutes behind in the overall classification gets a seven-minute lead,

that's a good breakaway for our team and we want the pack to let it go; it's a guarantee that one more day of the Tour de France will pass without the occurrence of anything dangerous to our team. A patron's team must also, at all costs, shelter its leader, never leaving him isolated among the other teams, without water or food, or forced to chase or work against the wind on his own.

The patron's part in this bargain is simpler, but also harder: be the strongest rider in the race, without question or a moment's falter.

From the beginning, we faltered — just the tiniest bit, and perhaps not even in a significant enough way to register with our rivals or the press and public, but I noticed it. And it put me on alert.

The opening time trial, what's known as the prologue, was short and hard, buffeted by the stiff winds common to northern France, and drenched by rain. Lance finished third — only four seconds down, but he'd told me beforehand he'd wanted to win. On the plus side, Ullrich had finished three seconds behind Lance. Over the course of the Tour, those few seconds would not mean much, but psychologically it gave the athletes an idea of where they stood.

Ullrich had won the Tour de France in 1998, and possessed such physical gifts and raw horsepower that Lance and I always considered him a threat — even when he didn't show up at the Tour in top shape, which was often. Ullrich had always seemed to ascribe to an older strategy of winning the Tour: he'd arrive a few pounds heavy and not in optimal shape, planning to use the early stages to ride into peak form. Lance and I believed you had to show up with your best game.

This year, it seemed that Ullrich had. He had a hard, chiseled look to his face, and the muscles of his legs and buttocks — the main power producers for cycling — seemed as if they'd been carved by a sculptor. The first time Lance and I got a glimpse of him at the Tour, we looked at each other and shook our heads. He'd brought his best, maybe enough to beat us.

Circumstances continued to tilt, ever so slightly, out of our favor. The first few stages were hillier than usual, and our team was working harder to control the race than they had the year before. In stage 4, a group of nine racers escaped on the rolling hills on the way to the town of Verdun and built a ten-minute lead. In the breakaway was Bobby Julich, who had finished third in the 1998 Tour and could climb and time trial well. We couldn't risk giving him that much time, so I directed the team to go to the front of the pack and chase full out—against a punishing coastal wind.

Eating up pavement like a rocket-powered steamroller, our team ended up literally cracking the pack in half: about eighty riders finished a full eighteen minutes ahead of another eighty riders. From the outside, our effort had been a tremendous show of force, a shining example of all that a patron's team should be. But once again, in secret, I was concerned. Though we showed a confident and energetic face in public, in the privacy of their hotel rooms and in the team bus and on the massage tables, the riders seemed achy, weary. They let their faces fall, looked drawn, tired. Their moods were listless rather than ebullient. The Tour was taking a huge toll on us.

I hoped that Verdun would be a good omen—that everything would turn around. We'd shattered the pack coming into it. It was where the team time trial was to start the next day. And it was the city where Lance had won the first Tour stage of his life, back in 1993.

In one sense, all the focus I'd put on the TTT paid off. Ullrich's team finished half a minute behind ours. We'd built a cushion between us and our most threatening opponent. But I had no chance to congratulate myself.

The stage, like the others before it, had been rainy and windy. As our team shot down the road, Vandevelde's wheel slipped on a painted road stripe—which become like ice when wet. He fell, sliding into one of his teammates, and before I could blink both of them were down, whirling across the slick road. Vandevelde broke his arm and would have to abandon the race. The other rider was banged up, bruised, sore, and achy, but vowed to pedal on.

Rain fell day after day. Wind howled in our faces. In stage 8, just before the race would enter the mountains, we made a critical mistake.

A group of fourteen riders had broken away early, and I decided not to order the team to chase. There were other squads that, logically, could not afford to let the breakaway succeed — Ullrich's German team, for one, couldn't afford to lose any more time. And the team of Joseba Beloki, a plucky, wiry Spaniard who'd finished third in 2000 and hoped to step onto the podium again this year, also should have wanted to squash the breakaway.

But those two teams, and all the others, dug their heels in. If there was any chasing to be done, they wanted it to be powered by our team. Maybe they'd become so used to us leading the charge there seemed to be no other option. Maybe they sensed our team was operating near its limit and hoped that one more long, hard chase would shatter us. It seemed as if they were willing to lose the Tour rather than take up the chase. I could not show that, once I'd made a decision, I could be manipulated into reversing it. We became locked in a tense, strategic standoff.

Meanwhile, the breakaway gained more and more time. The group ended up finishing thirty-six minutes ahead of the pack — the biggest lead in modern history. (There had been no lead bigger than twenty-two minutes since the early 1970s.)

Most of the riders who'd been in that group, some of whom were now up to half an hour ahead of Lance in the overall standings, were tactically meaningless. There were sprinters, flat-landers, kids, time-trial specialists — Lance, and Ullrich, would easily take back all that time from them once the race hit the mountains.

There was one racer who, I thought, might be trouble. Andrei Kivilev was a twenty-seven-year-old racer from Kazakhstan. He'd been far behind Lance in the standings, but with his thirty-six-minute gain now sat thirteen minutes ahead. I knew that he climbed well — nowhere near Lance's caliber, but maybe well enough to emerge from the mountains as the leader of the Tour de France.

Had we just lost the Tour? Vandevelde was gone. Another one

of our mountain goats had crashed in a different stage and could not fully use his left arm to support himself. The wind had taken a terrible toll on our entire team. I had confidence in Lance. He was still the strongest racer in the Tour. But I didn't think our team could protect him in the tough mountain stages to come. I didn't want Lance to be isolated, to ride alone mile after mile.

And I knew, from the way stage 8 had just unfolded, that the other teams would race not to win, but to make Lance lose. Ullrich and Beloki would not send their teammates out to chase down attacks; they would shadow Lance and either follow him as he did the hard work, or willfully sit back and engage in another standoff that would cost them their podium spots.

Our team was in a nearly unprecedented spot. Generally, you can always count on forming impromptu alliances on the road. The teams of the sprinters will help you control the pack or chase down breakaways on the flats, because they want to arrive at the finish in a position to launch their star to a stage win. Or maybe a team has someone in contention for the best young rider award, or has a chance to win the team award (given for the lowest total time of all their riders)—they will help you control the race. Riders who don't realistically think they have a shot at the overall victory but aspire to win second or third—an honor still guaranteed to bring respect, some measure of fame, and hundreds of thousands of dollars in sponsorship and contract money—will help out, too.

But Lance, and our team, had proved so dominating that it seemed the number one goal for the other teams was to make us lose, then to see if they could win: crack Lance's team, at any cost, then see if he can be shattered.

With Kivilev's cushion, and the state of our team, and Ullrich's spectacular form, and the determination of the other teams to see us lose, it was clear that our winning streak could end right here.

As Lance floundered on his bike, once more nearly falling off the back of the group as the mountain road grew steeper, a motorcycle TV crew pulled alongside the team car. A microphone was shoved into the open window, and as I drove I heard someone ask me what was wrong with my superstar.

I shrugged and said, "He will survive."

Again, the commentators' frantic shouts blared from the radio and TV: "The first mountain stage can tear the legs off any rider!"

They were right. The abrupt change from the relatively flat roads to the walls of the Alps and Pyrenees are always a shock to a rider's system. The pack has been hurling along flat roads for days, stretching out their legs to sprint then sitting back down and spinning again, flushing the waste byproducts out of their muscles. Then you hit that first slope and there's no more chance to recover, no place to take it easy, no use in trying to hide within the group. The steep angles of the mountains expose the riders who have been able to conceal less-than-perfect form. And sometimes, unaccountably, that first day of climbing is simply too big of a shock to even the fittest rider's system, and he will suffer a horrible, time-losing day of pain and humility—only to bounce back feeling fresh for the next stage but with too much damage done to his hopes for a high overall spot.

In the Tour, mountains are designated by five rankings, or categories, which describe how difficult the climb will be for the racers. It's a subjective ranking, of course, because part of the difficulty includes how many miles the racers have already done, how many climbs the whole day entails, how hard those other climbs are, the final elevation of the ascent, and even the anticipated weather or the condition or width of the road. The easiest climb is categorized as a 4, and the number scale goes up to 1. Speaking generally, a category 4 climb is something the riders will zip right over. A category 3 climb is around three miles long with an average grade of around 5 percent. (A 1 percent grade rises one foot for every one hundred feet it goes forward.) Category 2 climbs hit about 8 percent, without being much longer—it's a climb that would force most untrained, typical people to get off their bikes and start walking. A category 1 climb goes on for about twelve miles, with an average grade of at least 6 percent—so if you do some math you can figure out that a category 1 will gain about forty-five hundred to five thousand feet of elevation, or nearly a mile straight up. But remember there are five categories, not four. The toughest of them all is known as *hors categorie* (HC), or beyond classification. These are ascents considered so tough that the experience of racing up them cannot be captured by a number—the idea is infinite suffering. (In more concrete, though less glorious terms, an HC climb is generally about as long or slightly shorter than a category 1, but much steeper.)

Our first mountain stage in this 2001 Tour de France was full of HCs. It was a nightmare, around 130 miles long, and scaling three outside-category mountains. Worse, the peak of the last of the HCs was also the stage's finish: get dropped going up and you'd have no chance to catch back on during a descent.

There was one more thing: the finish was on Alpe d'Huez, a legendary, twelve-mile climb with twenty-one switchbacks that rose in front of you like a wall. Lance had always wanted to win on Alpe d'Huez. The great Italian *campionissimo*—champion of champions—Fausto Coppi had won on Alpe d'Huez. So had five-time Tour de France winner Bernard Hinault—the Badger. The tragic Italian racer Marco Pantani, who was blessed with immense talent but also so troubled that he died of a cocaine overdose in 2004, won twice on Alpe d'Huez, setting a record ascent time of 37:35 in 1997. More than half a million fans line the mountain's road. A victory atop Alpe d'Huez is a historical event. A kind of coronation.

But before we could even begin to worry about Alpe d'Huez, we had to make our way over the day's first two monsters: the Col de Madeleine and the Col du Glandon.

It was here, on the first one, the Madeleine, where Lance was mashing away at his pedals at the back of a dwindling pack being pushed ever harder by Ullrich and his team.

Chechu Rubiera, one of our few remaining climbers in full health and strength, drifted away from Lance's side and came back to the car. When I could see him through the open window on the driver's side, I said, "How goes it?"

Chechu looked around, a worried look on his face, making sure no other racers or media were nearby. We were all alone, but still, he leaned in. As quick as a finger snap, a smile flitted across his face then disappeared. "He's flying," Chechu whispered. "Lance is flying. Easy."

I suppressed my own grin. "Perfect," I said. With my eyes I motioned him back up to the pack.

"Horrendous!!!" screamed someone over the airwaves.

That was exactly what I wanted everyone to think.

Back in 2000, when I'd realized we were becoming the dominant team, I started trying to figure out what we would do when the other squads tried to turn our own strength against us. I knew I would be unable to count on making any allies at all.

But, I thought, what if I made some other team into an ally without their knowledge?

That was the birth of what has become known, famously, as the Bluff.

The idea was simple, really, once I'd found my way to it: no other team would help us if they thought our team was weak; they would wait, try to force us to grind ourselves into nothing, then attack Lance and see if he could be overcome when he was isolated. But, I realized, if other teams thought that Lance himself was weak, they would attack. They would take over the race. They would do the hard work at the front, imagining that they were about to pop Lance off the back at any second. They would set a hard pace that would keep the race in check—exactly what our team needed. As our de facto—albeit, unknowing—allies, some other team would deliver Lance safely to the foot of the mountains, where he could rocket past them.

I knew that what I was thinking of was a once-in-a-lifetime tactic; I could pull it out of our bag of tricks exactly once. After that, you would never be able to surprise anyone with the move again. I discussed the strategy with Lance on and off. He was averse to it. He always wanted to be the best, to show his dominance, to rule the race.

"If we do it," he said once, "it has to be because we have no choice."

"When the opportunity is perfect," I said.

So we waited. We waited, and we kept our own counsel.

Until the perfect opportunity arose.

More TV crews pulled up alongside me. Up ahead of us, Lance was grimacing. As another microphone was thrust into my face, I had a sudden realization: if Lance really were falling apart, I would try to project confidence. If I admitted that I was worried, it would be so out of character that the Bluff might be seen as being just that.

I needed to pull off the Bluff within the Bluff. I had to appear to be bluffing confidence to conceal my fear, when, in fact, I was bursting with pride that our strategy was working. It was one thing I hadn't thought of, or planned out.

I also realized I didn't want to lie outright.

So, very carefully, I leaned toward the microphone and told the world: "He looks bad, yes. But he is a champion."

That was all true.

As Ullrich and his team dragged the pack of the world's best riders behind them, their effort began to crack the race apart. Soon only twenty to thirty riders remained; Lance was always careful to remain near the back, or just off the back. I watched him dump water on himself.

We'd talked the night before about employing the Bluff, and earlier that day, he'd told me over the radio that he needed to come out of the pack and back to the car. I'd punched the gas, careened out on the left side of the road, and driven up toward the pack. When Lance had coasted back to the window, I looked out at him and knew what he was thinking. Simply, I'd said, "Maybe now is a time to show some weakness."

He'd nodded.

On and on he rode, hanging limp over his bike, puffing his chest in and out. Over the Madeleine. Up and over the Glandon.

A French racer, Laurent Roux, attacked at some point and gained minutes on the group, but Ullrich didn't care — he thought he had Lance dangling behind on the thinnest string, ready to snap.

As we approached Alpe d'Huez, I barked, "Lance!"

He soft-pedaled back to the car.

"One thing," I said. "When you go, you go *vollebak*."

Vollebak is Flemish, my native tongue, a language few people in the peloton understand. I'd taught Lance the word. It means all-out, 110 percent, over-the-top effort. He had to blow the Tour apart. I repeated: "*Vollebak*. You got it?"

When he's ready to pounce, Lance sometimes gets a wolfish look to his face. Today, he seemed full of glee. He smiled, and his eyes sparkled and for one second the costume of fatigue he cloaked himself in fell away. He said, "Johan, you're going to see *vollebak* like you've never seen *vollebak*."

At the foot of Alpe d'Huez, Roux had a seven-minute lead — the commentators were screaming that there was no way that lead could be erased in just twelve miles. Ullrich's team kept ratcheting up the pace, and all over the world, the live news was going out that Lance Armstrong was cracking.

"*Vollebak!*" I yelled into the team radio.

It was a beautiful thing to watch, Lance rising from his saddle, the choppiness instantly banished from his pedal stroke, the weight thrown off his shoulders. There was aggression and grace all at once, as if I was watching a cheetah bring down a gazelle. This was Lance in full power, and our plan in the glory of its bloom. The Tour de France had never seen anything like this American, or our strategy.

Rubiera, Lance, and Ullrich leapt up the road, immediately gapping the rest of the riders. Then Rubiera pulled off, and Lance stood. He looked back at Ullrich for what, in race time, was a long interlude but was perhaps two or three seconds — Ullrich, who, until that precise instant, had thought he was on his way to vanquishing Lance and winning the Tour.

Then Lance blasted away, as if he might tear the cranks off the bicycle.

"He's dropped!" I screamed ecstatically into Lance's ear. "Ullrich's dropped!"

I could hear the commentators in a fever pitch, but it was just noise. In front of us, the crowd of half a million fans parted like water driven to each side by the nose of a speedboat. But it was just color and movement to me. This moment, this act of sporting perfection, was all that really existed.

Lance caught Roux. He passed Roux, then raised his hands high, adding his name to the list of those who had won atop the legendary Alpe d'Huez.

He was the lion of the Tour de France, its patron, its unquestioned leader.

Of course the Tour de France was not over that day. Kivilev rode a courageous stage himself, finishing twelfth, only 4:39 behind Lance, maintaining around eight minutes of his lead over us.

In the end, Lance would take all that time and more back from Kivilev, as I knew he would after that day on Alpe d'Huez.

It is said that the yellow jersey is a golden fleece, and that he who wears it is charmed, blessed. Even approaching it confers great power. Kivilev rode as if *he* were a lion, holding on to his lead over Lance all the way to stage 13. It was another climbing stage, and it happened to cross the Portet d'Aspet, where Lance's teammate, Fabio Casartelli, had been killed in the 1995 Tour de France.

Lance won the stage and took the yellow jersey, dedicating both to Fabio. Kivilev hung on to finish fourth in Paris, just one step off the podium. A part of me always wished he'd been able to climb up there beside Lance; in 2003 Kivilev crashed during the Paris-Nice race and died of a head injury. For me, Kivilev has become tied in with the memories of that 2001 Tour. He was a rider who hid great strength inside a shell most experts predicted would be weak and easily crack. Lance, that year, was concealing the weakness of our team inside the suit of armor of his own fitness, then made everyone pay more attention to its imaginary chinks than its luster. When I compare them, I think I understand something important: strength and weakness live together, inside each of us, and we are fools if we do not see both when we look at someone else.

7

Lose a Little to Win a Lot

There are all kinds of ways to not finish first and still achieve victory.

LANCE'S DECISIVE 2001 VICTORY atop Alpe d'Huez—the melding of his supreme fitness and our strategic execution of the Bluff—was not our first encounter with the legendary mountain. Lance, that fabled climb, and I had a history together.

In 1999, the first year Lance won the Tour de France, stage 10 finished atop Alpe d'Huez. The previous day's stage, the race's first foray into the mountains, was when Lance had confirmed both his intention and his ability to not only make a comeback from cancer but become a Tour de France champion; the climbing specialists had been anticipating their chance to crack Lance, but he'd chased down a dangerous break by Fernando Escartín and Ivan Gotti, and left key rival (and my former teammate) Alex Zülle floundering in his wake. His performance that day solidified our hold on the yellow jersey, which he'd taken in the time trial right before the mountains.

The morning of stage 10, the entire team had adopted a heady, buzzy spirit that seemed equal parts inspiration, energy, and confidence. They wanted a repeat performance—to a man, they wanted once again to help Lance tear apart the pack in the mountains, show everyone we couldn't be beat. And it seemed clear that they would get what they wanted. Even then, barely halfway through our first Tour together, there was a feeling of inevitability about Lance's dominance. It was almost like the first time you hear a catchy song on the radio—you know it's going to be a hit.

That morning at breakfast, amid the joking and playful braggadocio, Lance and I found a moment alone. He said, "If I ride like yesterday, no one can beat me."

"That's true," I said. I nodded. I looked away for a moment, then took a deep breath and said, "Look, what did we come here for?"

"To win the Tour!" Lance answered immediately, a huge grin coming to his face, on top of that an expression of assuredness, then finally some amazement that our long-thought-about plans were coming to fruition. I felt some of that mysterious excitement coursing through my body: *We were living it! Finally! Maybe we'd been crazy when we'd talked about winning the Tour, and training on the routes instead of going to the other races the way you were supposed to—but we'd also been right!*

"We're here to win the Tour de France," I said. "That's right. The whole thing."

"The whole thing, Johan," Lance said.

"So we can't win today," I said flatly.

I'd been thinking all the previous night about what I had to tell Lance, and I knew he wouldn't want to hear it. In truth, *I* didn't want to hear it; the idea went against my own instinct, which was to say, "Let's go!" and charge ahead, taking every stage we could get. But I realized that that was how I would have reacted if I were racing. Then, winning a stage would have loomed as a major accomplishment in my career; there's no way I ever would have passed up such an opportunity. But with Lance, the stages were nothing more than steppingstones—each one was a piece of our strategy. Some were to gain time. Some were to intimidate rivals. Some were to recover. Some served simply to pass one more day without damage to our position, to get one stage closer to Paris. And some, like Alpe d'Huez, were most valuable if we used them to obscure our strategy and strength.

Lance had won the time trial by nearly a minute. The following day, he'd wiped the road clean on his way up Sestriere. I knew that physically, he could ride with the same level of power and intensity day after day, perhaps all the way to Paris. But I wasn't convinced that our young team—and our tiny staff of mechanics and masseurs—could handle the pressure of supporting an overwhelming favorite. I wanted a little less light thrown on our team, a little less heat and expectation. I wanted people to assume there was at least some doubt about Lance's ability to win.

The French media had started to describe Lance's performances as "superhuman" and "extraterrestrial," and I could read the suspicion and accusation between the lines. If we won again, so quickly, I could foresee that the media would bombard us with accusations of doping.

I also wanted to divert the attention of the other racers away from Lance, at least for a few stages: let them worry about each other for a while rather than giving every cyclist in the race no option but to concentrate on beating Lance.

"We're here to win for three weeks," I said. "Not three stages."

Lance frowned, his eyes narrowed, and a hard, stony look came to his face. But he listened as I talked. I understood that what I was telling him went against everything he was. Lance is one of the purest winners I have ever met. Whether it is riding a bike, or making a stock-market transaction, or arguing over who gets to treat the other to dinner, he wants to win. He needs to win. Victory is like oxygen to him.

"Trust me," I said. "You have to trust me again. Sometimes little losses are necessary for big wins."

Cycling is a fascinating sport when it comes to success. In sports such as soccer or basketball, there is a score. You either win or lose. But it's not so clear-cut in cycling. There are all kinds of ways to not finish first and still achieve victory—and I've always thought the sport is like life in that way. In the big multiweek stage races, you can end up fifth but still meet your goal of winning the jersey for best mountain climber. Or you can ride your team to tatters all day for what might seem to be no result to an outsider, while meanwhile you've safely transported your leader through a stage when he was sick, or you got him safely to the mountains, where he can shine. What appears to be a loss to outsiders can be the successful completion of your game plan.

To win on Alpe d'Huez that day, we didn't need to cross the finish line first. We needed to make sure that none of Lance's closest rivals got away from us and gained time. There were three key opponents we had to mark. Abraham Olano, a tough all-arounder from Spain, was in second place overall, about six minutes behind Lance. Zülle was nearly eight minutes back, but more dangerous to us than Olano. And, to guard against the outside chance of a dark horse winner, I thought we should watch Escartín as well, who was nine minutes back.

The best possible outcome for us would be that Lance could sit back and shadow those riders, while a climber far down in the standings escaped from the pack and won. There would be plenty of glory for that rider. It would be a big victory. And it would be a big break for us. All that attention would shine on someone else.

For our plan to work, we had to control the race right up to the base of the climb. We couldn't afford to risk letting someone too close to Lance get away during a chaotic stage. To minimize breakaways, almost from the gun I sent the team out hard, drilling them into the pavement, mile after mile at a pace so arduous that it discouraged almost everyone from trying to ride past us and escape. There were a few attempts at breakaways, a few solo launches or surprise moves from two and three riders at a time, but they never got far ahead before our grinding, relentless pace brought them back into the pack, as if we were reeling in the road like fishing line. It disappeared under the churning blue uniforms of our team.

Finally, Alpe d'Huez loomed before us. It is not a road that slithers up the mountain's side; it bounds forward, hopping up the mountain in a series of steep switchbacks; in each corner the slope steepens to a leg-withering degree, eases as the road traverses the mountainside, then, just before you feel a slight bit of relief in the hammering of your heart, the pavement leaps up again. Twenty-one times it does that.

At the first hint of rise, Lance's voice crackled over the radio: "Johan."

"Yes?"

"I could win this on a tricycle."

"I know."

I clicked the button a few times with my thumb. I said, "You know what to do."

Escartín attacked first. Lance very simply and very smoothly rode out of the pack and right up to the back of Escartín's wheel, spun the pedals around, and marked time. I could tell he was holding back. Zülle launched himself up the road, and Lance followed him too, then again sat calmly just behind his rival's bike. The pace rose, again and again. Riders began to come off the back, and soon there was only a tiny, select group of the best climbers on the planet, churning up a mountain that had stood there long before they had existed and would be there long after.

From my spot behind this elite pack, I recognized the colors on the jersey of one of the riders who began faltering: Olano. He was letting tiny gaps open between his bike and the others—at first just a few inches, then half a foot, then he was two feet behind the group. He was done.

"Olano is gone," I said to Lance.

Within a few miles the pack was even more select. It was just Zülle, Lance, and two or three others. With about three miles to go, I noticed some movement at the back of the pack and saw a lean figure stand and begin to rock his bike from side to side between his pistoning legs, maximizing the leverage. It was Giuseppe Guerini, and he was attacking.

I knew him—he was a wonderful climber. And he was fifteen minutes behind Lance in the standings.

"Here comes Guerini," I told Lance. "This one's good for us."

Go, I thought to myself. *Win it. Make Alpe d'Huez yours.*

And he did—though it was not without drama. Near the top, a spectator wielding a camera stepped in front of Guerini. The two of them smashed to the ground. Guerini shook himself free, leapt to his feet, threw his leg over his bike, and was moving up the road again in seconds—just one more example of the chaos of the Tour de France. Even with the crash, none of our rivals could stay on Guerini's wheel, and Lance never tried; he simply followed the group up the hill and finished fifth—a victory. A stunning victory, really, though we could tell no one about it.

The pressure was not off us. We were still an incredible story, a worldwide sensation. But internally, in terms of race strategy, we'd carved out a little relief for ourselves. For a few days we would be regarded by our rivals—racers and team directors alike—with slightly less intensity. In that brief period, we rested as much as we could. Riders who'd been stuck in the pack began skirmishing for stage wins, and the day's glory went to racers such as David Etxebarria, Salvatore Commesso, Dimitri Konyshev—all great riders, but none of them a threat for the overall win. With just that little bit of reprieve, our team was able to once again spend time at the front of the race, surrounding Lance and keeping away from the chaos of the middle of the pack, far from the crashes and ready to follow any attack his rivals might make. But those attacks never came. Escartín did make a courageous breakaway for a win in a later mountain stage, in the Pyrenees, but I instructed Lance to let him go, to instead shadow Zülle; I wasn't worried about Escartín's overall chances anymore, because I knew he'd lose a lot of time in the stage 19 time trial. (His mountain victory brought him to just over six minutes behind Lance, but he did, as I'd counted on, fade to 10:26 back by the end of the Tour.) Zülle himself never got closer than 7:30.

Even those who most closely followed Lance's career, even all the experts who pick apart the races on TV—you never hear any of them talk about the 1999 Alpe d'Huez stage. To the rest of the world, Lance did nothing but ride in the pack. To me, that's the day that just might have saved the entire Tour de France for us, the day that I learned you can win without anyone ever knowing it happened.

8

Recruit Too Much Talent

*The greatest athletes, academics, politicians—you
name it—could not stretch to the heights they reach
if they did not stand on a foundation that was as solid
as they were stellar: a great team.*

L ANCE AND I used to joke that we weren't so much worried
about what teams we might lose to, but about the team that
we'd lost.

If you could somehow gather together into a single squad all
the racers who've left our team, that roster would rack up one of
the world's most impressive list of victories; our "ex-team" would
be better than most current teams. From 1999—the first full season Lance and I worked together—until the team disbanded at
the end of 2007, racers who left us won the Tour of Italy, the Tour
of Spain, the world championship, Paris-Roubaix, Ghent-Wevelgem, Paris-Nice, two Tours of Flanders, Liège-Bastogne-Liège,
three Tours of Romandie, the Tour of Luxembourg, the Dauphiné
Libéré, two Olympic medals, several national championships
around the world, the Tour of California, the Tour of Georgia, the
leader's jersey in all three of the Grand Tours (France, Italy, and
Spain), and multiple stages in all three Grand Tours as well.

I always regarded that growing list of palmarès as a sign not of
our failure but of our success. We didn't have a talent drain. We
had a talent overflow. That's a pretty good problem to have.

As a kid in Belgium, I rode my bike everywhere and dreamed of winning the Tour de France—though not as a team director!

My father—my most ardent fan and my biggest inspiration—died five weeks before I raced the Tour de France with ONCE in 1993.

As a director, I guided my teams to more than ninety yellow jerseys (Lance himself wore eighty-three), but I claimed my own in Stage 7 of the 1995 Tour.

Here I am winning my only yellow jersey—by being the only racer out of the whole pack who was able to stay with the legendary Miguel Indurain, then pass him at the line.

In the 1996 Tour, I skidded in a corner and rode off a hundred-foot cliff—then scrambled back up to finish the stage, a feat that for years brought me more fame than anything else.

After Lance made his comeback from cancer and I convinced him he could win the Tour, we spent the spring alone, training in the Alps—a crazy idea that paid off.

A rare moment of calm inside my rolling office, where I plot strategy, watch the race on the dash-mounted TV, radio instructions to the team, and answer my mobile phone—while driving at breakneck speed on narrow roads.

A mechanic hangs out of the window to make a rolling repair—a bold maneuver, considering I'm the one at the wheel.

HOPE

COU2AGE

PERS3VERANCE

WIS4OM

INTE5RITY

DE6TINY

MAG7C

In 2003, before Lance won his fifth Tour de France, I saw this screensaver on his laptop. Even back then, he was thinking about winning seven—not just his fifth—and, from that moment on, so was I.

On the final stage of Lance's last Tour de France, in 2005, we took a moment for the traditional rolling toast of champagne—the end of one era, and the start of a new one.

Five years after he left our team to lead another, Levi Leipheimer returned to work with me—and won the 2007 Tour of California. He then climbed to a career-best third in the Tour de France.

At our pre-season training camp in 2007, Alberto Contador told me that he wanted to win Paris-Nice. It was a brash statement, but he made good on his word, winning the prestigious stage race on the last day.

Alberto Contador and I take a victory lap on the Champs Élysées in Paris, moments after his 2007 Tour de France win—his first, and my eighth in nine years.

As the entire team stood atop the podium at the end of the 2007 Tour, I was filled with jubilation and satisfaction—and the knowledge that as a team we had accomplished all we could.

After retiring from the Discovery team, all I really knew about the future was that I wanted to stay in cycling, but only in a way that let me spend more time with my wife, Eva Maria, and daughter, Victoria.

From the very beginning of my career as a team director, I understood that even Lance could not win consistently—year after year—without an all-star roster surrounding him. The greatest athletes, academics, politicians—you name it—could not stretch to the heights they reach if they did not stand on a foundation that was as solid as they were stellar: a great team. I made it a top priority to discover and recruit talent, whether it was up-and-coming kids or seemingly worn-out veterans who I thought could blossom again if exposed to the unique mix of work ethic, strategies, and focus our team had mastered. Primarily, of course, signing the best riders made us strong on the road; workhorses such as George Hincapie, Viatcheslav Ekimov, José Rubiera, and others were willing to sacrifice their chances at individual wins by chasing down attacks, driving the pace high mile after mile, or withering our opponents' legs by setting a fierce pace up climbs (until they blew up and had to pull off, letting another teammate take over). Secondarily—and quite calculatingly—signing top riders to our team meant that they would be racing for us rather than against us: much better to have a former (or future) winner of the Tour of Italy helping Lance up the mountains than to worry about when he was going to attack us. The third reason, which felt distant at many times in my career—but never insignificant—was that I knew someday the team would have to find a way to win without Lance. Though no one could ever fill those legendary shoes, I was committed to auditioning people for the role.

In fact, one of the criteria I used when hiring my assistant sport directors was their ability to spot talent. Dirk Demol, a Belgian who'd won Paris-Roubaix, was the first person to tell me I should make sure I found a way to watch a kid named Alberto Contador race—years before Contador would end up winning the Tour de France for us in 2007. Another assistant director who had an eye for talent was Sean Yates, a bright, funny Englishman who'd ridden as a pro for fourteen years, from 1982 to 1996, had won a stage in the Tour and worn the yellow jersey, and had ridden with Lance way back in the early and mid-1990s, when they'd both been on the Motorola team. Yatesy, as he's called, is generally acknowledged as one of the sport's all-time great descenders; for this reason he's still respected and beloved by even the youngest pros, and he always seemed to know which of the novice riders were destined for success. At the end of 2006 I hired Eki—longtime, loyal racer Viatcheslav Ekimov—as our final assistant team director.

All of those guys were capable of leading the teams in the races I couldn't be at, but I don't think I would have hired any of them strictly for that. I needed lots of eyes out there looking for talent. There was no way I could do it alone. To understand why, you have to know a little bit about what the job of team director entails.

Think of me as the ringmaster of a traveling circus. From 1999 until I retired at the end of 2007, I was on the road an average of 200 days a year, and never less than 180. Most of that time was spent at races or training camps, or getting to and from races and training camps. So nearly everything I did—from designing the race schedule, to setting up training plans, to signing new riders, to recruiting, all the way down to such details as approving the order for all the energy bars and gels we'd need that season—happened on the road. I have a room at home in Madrid, Spain, that serves as an office. But my real office was in the driver's seat of a car, in the aisle seat of an airplane, at the keyboard of my Black-Berry.

The rest of the staff was nearly as decentralized. We had one office in Belgium, which was staffed by five assistants who handled the team's logistics: that's where we ordered, received, and stored everything we needed to run a team—from the clothing for twenty-eight racers and forty staff members, to all the bike parts, all the food, water bottles, massage tables, towels, travel cases for the bikes, and even the stickers and photos we handed out to kids and fans. We also stored the trucks, cars, and buses that we used to drive to the races in Europe. There was another office in Austin, Texas, that served both as the headquarters for the team's management (some investors, Lance, his agent Bill Stapleton, and me) and as a logistical outlet for our U.S. races. In all, there were just over seventy people working for the team, around sixty-five of whom somehow reported upstream to me. We had to have, of course, the routine organizational and planning meetings that you'd expect for any business of that size, complicated by the fact that the four directors and I, plus a couple mechanics and a couple *soigneurs* (in pro cycling parlance, this is a caregiver who is something of a cross between a masseuse and a valet), had to be at each race, not to mention three or four squads of five to ten riders who traveled separately to the various events. My mobile phone would ring at six in the morning, and at 2:00 A.M. I would make my last call or send my last message. The schedule, the pace, the unpredictability—riders could crash at any time, forcing us to choose a replacement who we'd been counting on for another race in another country, or the team bus would get a flat and be a day late making it from Belgium to Switzerland—was not consuming; it was obliterating.

Yet, through everything, I never lost sight of the importance of recruiting talent. I knew the whole organization would come crashing down if we didn't have that foundation. Dirk, Sean, and Eki worked at the street level, helping us sign riders such as Vladimir Gusev, who at twenty-three won the best climber jersey in the Tour of Switzerland, and Janez Brajkovic, who at twenty-two won the Tour of Georgia (and, simultaneously, its best young rider jersey).

There was one episode that proved to everyone the depth and authenticity of my commitment to recruiting talent.

Going into the 2003 season, I kept thinking about Max Van Heeswijk, a veteran racer who I'd thought had a lot of promise when he broke into the pro ranks back in 1995 when I was still racing. For some reason, in the years since then Max had never lived up to his potential and gotten a reputation as a sort of underachieving, difficult rider. Now, I'd heard that his contract negotiations had broken down, and it appeared that no one wanted to hire him. I figured I could sign him for a relatively small salary, revive his original spark, and end up with a valuable addition to the team. I knew he had a world-class engine still sitting somewhere inside him. I was confident that our team could tune it back up.

There was one problem: we didn't have a dime left in our budget. All of our negotiations for the year had closed, and our team was signed, set, and fully stocked. I had a meeting with the team management, the accountants, the owner, the various board members, including Lance. I explained who Max was, what he'd accomplished in his career, and that I was sure he would blossom under our leadership.

"This is a great opportunity," I finished up. "I know him. I'll vouch for him. He is a great talent. And he's very cheap this year."

We didn't have a single dollar left for salaries, the board explained.

"We need this guy," I said, pressing.

Sorry, the board said.

Impulsively, I said, "Take it from my salary."

"You're crazy!" said Lance.

"We pay him out of my salary," I said. "He's on the team."

There was silence. Stunned silence.

I'd always told other people—and myself—that I didn't do my job for the money. I want to be well paid, of course, but I've never thought of money as one of my prime motivators. It's more like a very welcome accompaniment—I'm glad that success in cycling has meant that I could secure the future for my family, see the world, live in a beautiful home in a beautiful city. But, I always said, I love what I do—winning—and that love came before money, before security, before thoughts of health insurance or pensions or anything like that. And there was the proof that day: as I stood there and stubbornly offered part of my own salary to hire a racer I believed could help us win, I felt great about what I'd done.

I just wished I'd told my wife first.

I ended up using about 10 percent of my year's salary to pay Max—and after just one year in our program, he had the best season of his life, taking more than ten victories and wearing the leader's jersey at three separate multiday races. It was a rebirth beyond even what I had imagined, the second biggest career resuscitation I'd ever been a part of. (A certain cancer survivor from Texas will be tough to dethrone from number one.)

My reward? After I'd not only taken a gamble on Max when no one else would, but used my own, personal money to fund that chance—and then successfully revived his cycling career—he began fielding offers from other teams, then used those offers to re-open his contract with us.

I'm old enough, and experienced enough, to understand that when it comes to business—which pro cycling is—loyalty is a luxury rather than a necessity. But I have to admit that such a swift turn away from my generosity stung me. Lance still likes to tell me I'm crazy for using my own money—and crazier still for not seeing the fallout coming. All I know is that I wouldn't go back in time and undo the deal if I were given the chance. For one thing, it's not a bad idea for your colleagues to think you have a little craziness inside you when it comes to how far you'll go to build a winning team. For another thing: I was right. We were a better team thanks to Max. Being right—and being ready to stand behind my belief with my own money—gave me a new kind of weight, a new kind of authority, in all those years afterward, when I talked about what I thought our team needed, whether it was certain riders or new bike designs or even new jersey colors.

And anyway, in truth—aside from the times I personally funded their career rebirths—it was never much of a surprise when riders left for other teams. We had become so adept at finding, recruiting, and developing cyclists into top talents that it sometimes felt as if other squads saw us as a kind of farm team. I knew that was the price we had to pay for our aggressive program. I also understood that we were so successful at creating the conditions that allowed riders to learn and flourish that we turned them into cyclists capable of being leaders on other teams—and that many of them would then want that chance. That felt normal to me, a natural parallel to how much of the world works, whether it's the salesman who leaves to start his own company or the parent who instills in his children the knowledge they need to go out on their own. Our program gave many riders their first taste and full understanding of what it takes to be a top pro. From their first day at their first camp with us, every single rider was given a schedule that outlined how their training programs overlay with the races we anticipated them participating in. They understood which races represented their chance to be one of our team leaders, and in which races we'd be counting on them to play the valuable support roles. We were not an organization that dictated a racer's diet or sleep habits or social schedule—but we made it clear that each rider was expected to do all those things in the most professional way that made sense for them. (And we paired veteran riders with rookies to help pass along that knowledge.) Most cycling teams were not run with this combination of precision and passion; they were more old school, run on the emotions of how the team director felt the week he made out a training schedule, or traditions about which riders had raced where in the past, friendships between riders who wanted to travel and race together, or national pride that, for instance, might ensure that all of a team's Frenchmen were going to do a race in France no matter what sort of balance that gave them between sprinters and climbers.

We were like a leader factory, and out went our products through the doors, year after year!

I'm not claiming it wasn't frustrating—for me as well as for the riders who left. It seemed as if some of them had to get themselves to an agitated or disgruntled state to find the impetus they needed to leave the team. The elements that had helped them grow as cyclists—our team's discipline, the work ethic, the clear hierarchy, the long-term scheduling—could come to be interpreted as chaffingly overly restrictive or hyperregimented. I've taken my fair share of criticism from some of the riders who went to other teams. Some of them have told stories about how I didn't equally distribute our best equipment, but saved it for our strongest racers. In other cases, riders who had been clearly told they had made the roster for the Tour de France in a support role were unhappy because, to save their strength for an upcoming stage when I thought Lance would benefit more from their help, I ordered them not to ride as well as they could even if they thought they could win that day.

I never held those criticisms against those riders. For one thing, I always did do whatever it took to make our team as a whole stronger—even if it meant forcing some riders to accept individual sacrifices. For another thing, I always thought that, even with a new job and a shot at leadership waiting, it had to be pretty hard to talk yourself into leaving our team—we were the most successful, most professionally run, most well-known cycling team on the planet. Our riders (and staff) could almost count on receiving five- or even six-figure bonuses from the prize earnings we would accumulate throughout the year. I tried to remind myself that those complaining riders were somehow just doing what they needed to do to make a break, and that deep down they knew, and appreciated, how our team had helped them develop.

That's not to say I didn't feel great when the whole process went exactly right.

I don't think I'd ever seen Levi Leipheimer outside of race videos or pictures before we signed him to our team for the 2000 season. He was strictly a domestic U.S. racer, and our paths had never crossed. But I liked the scouting reports I'd gotten: he was twenty-six, had won the U.S. time-trial championship in 1999, and seemed to still be undeveloped, both physically and in terms of his cycling skill and knowledge. Like with me, it seemed, early lab results showed that he had a pro engine but probably not an exceptional one the way Lance or the other great champions did. When we talked on the phone a few times before he officially joined the team, I thought he was quiet, almost studious, with a polite manner and a questioning nature. At the time, I'd only guided Lance to victory in that one Tour de France, earlier that year, but I could sense in Levi's manner—perhaps the serious questions he asked, or the way he rarely questioned my answers to his questions—a respect but not awe for me and for the sport.

In the spring of 2000, we had our first training camp in Avila Beach, California, near San Luis Obispo. A skinny kid—not muscularly lean in the way the top pros were, but having something more like the stringiness of a teenager—with sandy hair atop pleasantly neutral features walked over to me, stuck out his hand, and said, "I'm Levi." I liked him immediately for that small, open gesture. I'm not sure why.

He turned out to be stronger than I'd anticipated but, I think, not as strong as he'd hoped. I kept him almost exclusively on a domestic schedule—I wanted him to get a lot of experience racing, and I thought that if I took him over to Europe too soon he'd simply suffer and get dragged along with the pack rather than being able to try out various strategies. He had a natural, streamlined riding style that made for a good time trialist, and as he added muscle he started to drop the skinniness without gaining much weight. His power-to-weight ratio was improving, and he started hanging out at the front of the climbs when we trained. There was something else that was more impressive: he was not afraid to ask for advice from anyone he thought might be able to help him. If another rider on the team had ridden a course that was on Levi's schedule, he'd ask about the roads, the climbs, where the breakaways had happened. He'd ask the racers why they ate certain things, then ask the cook how it was prepared. He peppered me with queries about cadence, pedaling styles, various race strategies. He asked Lance about everything. And every answer he got, he took in with that respectful, serious but somehow quietly affable attitude I'd first felt when I talked to him on the phone.

At the end of that first season, he came to me one day and said, "I want to ask you something."

"Okay," I said, smiling because I knew what he was going to ask. Almost all riders asked the same thing eventually.

"What do I have to do to make the Tour de France team next year?"

Although the question was always the same, I always gave each racer a different answer—a real one, though I tried to be encouraging as well as honest. "The way we are racing," I said as I placed my hand on Levi's shoulder, "I don't see how you can make it next year. The way the team is built I don't see a hole for you to fill. And I think you need more experience. In the Tour de France I think it would just be trouble for you. You will be better in the Tour of Spain."

I'd been more honest than encouraging this time, on a hunch, and I looked into Levi's eyes, but they didn't waver. He nodded his head. He said, "Thanks," and I had the feeling that he actually meant it.

I kept to my word the next year and put Levi into the Tour of Spain. Our designated leader was Roberto Heras, who had won the race in 2000, and I asked Levi to ride as his lieutenant. It was a big responsibility. Three times, during the first three time-trial stages, Levi leapt ahead of Heras (a lean climber without much ability to do well in time trials) in the overall standings. But after each stage he dutifully went back to work for Heras, helping him in the mountains as best he could. It was a completely unselfish effort.

After twenty days of racing, with just one stage left, Heras was in third, 2:20 behind the leader, Oscar Sevilla. Levi was in fifth, 3:55 back, a remarkable result considering that he'd been forced to burn so much energy working for Heras. Levi had given us a great ride, but there seemed to be little to celebrate: the last stage was another time trial, and it was almost certain that Heras would lose his spot, and that though Levi might do well he probably couldn't make up enough time to finish on the podium.

Averaging nearly 30 mph on the twenty-eight-mile course, Levi leapfrogged into third place overall.

I was surprised, proud, happy for him—and sad. I knew his time to leave our team had come. Other teams would court him, offering him more money, which we could give him, but there were two things we couldn't give: a role as the team leader and the chance to ride for the podium in the Tour de France. It was simple: unless Lance happened to crash or somehow couldn't compete in

July, Levi wouldn't get a shot at the yellow jersey on our team for at least another five years.

He and I acknowledged as much when we spoke before he left to join Rabobank in 2002.

I wished him luck. "But not against us," I said.

"You know, this is because I want to lead," he said.

"You're doing the right thing," I said, meaning it. "I'd like to have you back some day, though."

"As the leader," Levi said.

We shook hands, parting just as we'd first met.

Levi finished in the top ten of the Tour de France three times in the next four years. (He crashed out in 2003.) Whenever we'd run into each other at races, he was friendly and funny, and he still regarded me with that initial respect. After Tom Danielson outdueled him on the final half mile of Brasstown Bald to win the Tour de Georgia in 2005, Levi had come over and said, "Nice job. You got me." He switched teams again, winning the Dauphiné Libéré in 2006 — the first American to do so since Lance in '03. In the Tour de France that year, he had a poor time trial and a bad day in the first mountain stage, and ended up thirteenth overall, his lowest finish ever. But to my eye, he was still the same studious, professional, genuine rider I'd noticed so long ago — only stronger. Lance had retired the year before, and I needed a new team leader.

I called Levi. I said, simply, "How would you like to be on the podium of the Tour de France in 2007?"

And I didn't even have to spend my own money to bring him back.

9

Trust People — Not Products

Technology can help you win. So can a team bus. A solid recruiting program. An inspiring mission statement. But none of those things actually do the winning. A million dollars can't ride a bicycle. Neither can a million bits of data. Races aren't contested in wind tunnels. It's people who perform.

T O A LOT OF casual fans of cycling, it might seem ludicrous that, in a race that lasts nearly an entire month, covers more than two thousand miles, and takes more than eighty hours of pedaling, teams will spend, say, ten thousand dollars for a wheel that might save eight seconds over the old one. The scale appears to be laughably out of whack, the return on investment pitiful. Yet it is in such minuscule margins of technology that champions search for an edge over their opponents. Find eight saved seconds in a wheel, three in a new skinsuit, one in a water bottle, ten from streamlined shoes, and suddenly you're looking at a more significant number.

Lance and I got a real-world example of this in the 2003 Tour de France. At the end of that race, after eighty-three hours of total racing time, Lance's margin over Jan Ullrich when they both strode up the podium in Paris was a mere sixty-one seconds. That was too close for us — an insecure advantage no matter how we looked at it. For instance, that's two-hundredths of 1 percent of the time they spent on their bikes that July. Think of it this way: if Lance had been given a sixty-one-second head start, then he and Ullrich had raced along at 20 mph for all of the Tour's 2,077 miles, the gap between them would have been just five football fields at the end. Here's another sobering comparison of how close we came to being defeated: at Lance's average power output—measured in watts (or horsepower, one of which is equal to 746 watts)—Ullrich would have beat us if he'd been able to produce just 0.03 more horsepower.

The simplest way to think of those sixty-one seconds: it was our smallest cushion ever. Lance had won in 1999 by 7:37; in 2000 by 6:02; in 2001 by 6:44; and in 2002 by seven minutes flat.

No Tour de France is ever safe until the champion is holding up flowers and kissing the podium girls on the Champs Élysées. Anything can happen, right up until the end: A crash. An equipment malfunction. The flu. The fragility of the leader's hold on the yellow jersey is part of the miracle of winning it multiple times. But, going into the final stages each year with around six minutes to spare, we knew we could afford an untimely flat or a minor run of bad luck. The hard, unpredictable stages in the mountains and time trials were customarily finished by then, and it would be nearly impossible for a rival to escape on the final flat stages and gain much time.

Safeguarding a sixty-one-second lead, however, was a different story. If a cat darted out from a farmer's field and created mayhem in the pack—and it has happened—we could easily lose a minute if Lance crashed. If some freak mechanical occurrence befell us at just the wrong time—say a shift or brake cable snapped at the start of a series of rollers—a hard attack might be able to gain that minute back. A spectator could step into the road to snap a photo and knock Lance over.

In Paris, at the end of that Tour de France in 2003, the sweat had barely dried on Lance's body and our smiles were still in strong evidence when he said to me, "That was too close."

"Never again so close," I said.

In a way, that narrow victory was the best thing that could have happened to us that year. Lance was now a five-time winner — tying him for the record with Miguel Indurain, Bernard Hinault, Eddy Merckx, and Jacques Anquetil. It seemed inevitable that we now had to focus on winning six, with all the pressure that comes with breaking a hallowed, long-standing sports record. Since the Tour began in 1903, no one had ever won six. Fans whispered of a curse that stopped the hopeful at five. Pseudo-experts talked of how five wins took such a terrible toll on the body that no human could withstand a sixth win. Historians pondered the improbability that any racer could avoid a serious crash or serious illness for so many years in a row, and posited that in year six our luck was bound to balance out.

Those sixty-one meager seconds showed us the way to victory next year: we would ignore all the hype about records and history and luck and curses, and dedicate ourselves to the simple pursuit of winning big again. We wanted to once again dominate the biggest, hardest, most famous, wildest bicycle race in the world. That was the only thing that would really feel like a win to us.

Lance and I agreed immediately that we wanted to ratchet up the intensity on our race preparation for 2004 — once we found out what the race route was, we'd identify the key stages and relentlessly train on them. We'd take more of the team to more of the roads that would be in the Tour. We'd know those race roads so well we'd see each pebble and paint stripe in our sleep. Lance vowed that his training and diet would take on a new focus, too. He'd always been fanatical about his own preparation; now his training was going to be taken to near-insane levels. As he told me about the workouts and days he had planned, I knew that he'd be training harder than most other pro cyclists rode when they raced.

There was only one weakness left in our program: gear.

During the Tour, there had been a lot of press and a lot of talk among the racers about Ullrich's time-trial bike. It was said to be the fastest bike in the world — when tested in a wind tunnel, it was more aerodynamic than any other. Lance and I didn't know if this was true. And if there was an aerodynamic advantage, we didn't know how big a part it had played when Ullrich beat Lance in the stage 12 time trial that year (when Lance, dehydrated, had ceded 1:36 to Ullrich).

But the buzz Ullrich's bike received made us think about our own approach to gear. And we came to a surprising conclusion. Lance had always insisted on having the best: A bike that rode just the way he wanted it to (stiff and fast). His shoes were custom-made to fit his feet. The edges of helmets were shaved to match his judgments about comfort and fit. On shorts and jerseys and skinsuits, seams were moved around to make him more comfortable. From socks to glasses to gloves to water bottles, we exhaustively analyzed every detail and molded each piece of gear to maximize Lance's performance. But despite that fanaticism, we uncovered a weakness in our approach: although we examined and customized every piece of gear we used, we did so in a separate process for each item. There'd never been any effort to figure out how all of Lance's gear worked in concert.

In past years, we had noticed and worked around some small incompatibility problems. One year, for example, a helmet from Giro and eyeglasses from Oakley just didn't feel comfortable when used together. Now, I realize that to many people it sounds silly to focus on what might seem to be such monumentally unimportant details as how the top edge of the frame of a pair of sunglasses occasionally bumps the bottom edge of a helmet, or how the arms of sunglasses slightly lose their grippiness when the straps of a helmet come between them and the side of the head. But you have to understand that it's precisely that insane level of attention to detail that helped Lance achieve what no human in history ever had — those seven consecutive victories in the most chaotic and unpredictable sporting event on earth. Whether it was obsessing about the thickness of Lance's race socks, or which switchback would be the best one to launch an attack during the last climb of a 120-mile stage, he and I had always bore down with our full focus on every element we could think of. In the beginning, of course, we'd been limited somewhat by money, but as Lance had continued winning Tours and our budgets had grown we were able to test more bikes, request more prototypes. All of the world's top riders had similar programs — Ullrich's time-trial bike was just one example. But none of them, including us, we realized, had ever studied every piece of gear — from socks to bike frame — as a whole unit. That could be our edge.

"What if we tried that?" I asked Lance. "What if we got all the equipment sponsors together, got them to share designs."

"Like a team," Lance said.

"It'll be tough," I warned him. Some of the companies that designed our products were competitors in certain areas. They might balk at cooperating, sharing resources, maybe even divulging unproven, secret technology.

"Johan," Lance said, "we live for tough."

So it was that just two weeks after the Tour de France had ended, Lance and I started telling our contacts at Trek, Giro, Nike, and Oakley what we had planned. It wasn't so much a question as a statement of intent: we're doing this — jump on. In September, everyone met in San Francisco, at the office of Thom Weisel, our team's chairman.

Besides representatives from our major sponsor companies, Lance and I had recruited other experts — big names in the technology field, such as Steve Hed, one of the world's leading researchers into aerodynamics. Behind the scenes, there was even more support. For instance, though Giro had assigned a lead designer to help with our helmets, there was a team of a dozen more people assisting him. The Nike team was just as big. There had never been an effort like this in all of cycling — and to celebrate the fact, someone came up with the idea of calling our program F-One, after the multimillion-dollar development initiatives that went into every Formula 1 racing team.

"I like that," Lance, the fan of all things fast, said.

• • •

The first thing our F-One team did was send Lance's bike for study at a wind tunnel at the University of Washington. We also bought, and brought along, as many other pro time-trial bikes as we could find — including a version of Ullrich's special, much-hyped Walser bike. Giro showed up with ten helmets. Nike brought several versions of an aerodynamic skinsuit that used ultraslick fibers, dimples (like a golf ball), and other tricks to cheat the wind.

Because we didn't want to interrupt Lance's training, we used a body double to test all the equipment. A forty-one-year-old triathlete from Vancouver named John Litherland turned out to have nearly the same body dimensions as Lance, right down to the slight hump both riders got in their backs when they were arched forward over their handlebars. I think of him as one of the unheralded heroes of Lance's seven Tour victories. For hour after hour, Litherland curled over various arrangements of bikes and handlebars as the giant fan of the wind tunnel blew a 35-mph gale in his face.

We found out that a rider on Ullrich's Walser was indeed more aerodynamic than on Lance's current bike. Our experts tinkered, calculated, ran computer programs, made adjustments a millimeter at a time, repositioned helmets. Litherland held his wrists flat, curved down, moved his shoulders forward and crouched down low over the bike, stuck his arms forward — whatever we asked.

By December, we were ready for Lance. The F-One program had come up with a new bike that, like Ullrich's, had a very narrow bottom bracket, which is the part of the frame that the cranks (which hold the pedals) fit through. This brought a rider's feet closer together, which seemed to be a big aerodynamic advantage. The bike also had a slightly more horizontal hand position. There was a new time-trial helmet that seemed nearly invisible to onrushing winds, and a skinsuit that posted the fastest numbers anyone had ever seen.

"Look at these numbers," Steve Hed said when Lance arrived. The bike's drag — its resistance as it moved against air — was minuscule, which was good: the lower the drag, the faster the bike.

Some of the experts, including Len Brownlie of Aerosports Research, were saying they'd never seen better numbers. Some people were saying this was the fastest bike in the world.

Lance walked into the wind tunnel, bent down, and began putting on his cleated shoes. There was an almost reverent silence, as if we were in a chapel. He swung a leg over the bike, took a few strokes, rolled his shoulders around, and settled down into his riding position. The big, loud turbines driving the fans started up, and we could hear nothing.

On the floor in front of Lance, there was a projection of the key performance data the computers in the control room were tracking. He could see instantaneous feedback about his watts, his heart rate, the bike's drag, and other important numbers. There it was: the bike was faster.

Lance was on the fastest bike in the world.

Nobody is really sure what the entire program cost — figuring out the total salaries, development costs, materials, travel, and all the related expenses turned out to be impossible. Most of us estimated that the entire cost of the program, including every company and outside expert, and our own team's time and investment, easily exceeded $1 million.

Lance wasn't riding a million-dollar bike, but the F-One team had spent that much to get him on that particular bike, in that specific position, wearing those specific clothes.

"I like it," Lance said. "But . . ."

There was silence.

"Something's funny about my power output."

What good, I thought, *is the fastest bike in the world without the fastest man in the world?* I studied Lance pedaling, that familiar cadence I must have watched literally millions of times, those feet swiping circles around and around and around. Was there something slightly different about his stroke, or was I imagining things?

We took the bike out of the wind tunnel — because what good is the fastest bike in the world if it never touches a road?

In February 2004 Lance won a time trial on the new bike at the

Tour of Algarve, in Portugal. But at the finish, he said, "I should have really killed this field. I could feel my power dropping off. Something's not right."

I could see, as he rode the new bike, what I thought I might have been imagining before: he was, ever so slightly, laboring on the bike. It was the kind of blip that was imperceptible unless you'd spent as much of your life watching Lance pedal as I had.

In March, he raced the new bike in Spain at the Tour of Murcia, and finished fifth in a time trial. "My hips hurt," he said. "I'm thinking about trying a race on the old bike."

That April, at the Tour of Georgia, we set up Lance's old bike with the new handlebar and riding position. He won the time trial and was bursting with energy and enthusiasm when he said, "That, Johan, felt great."

I knew what he was telling me: there was no way he was going to ride the million-dollar bike. We'd tested a lot of crazy ideas in the program. There was something we called the ice vest that Lance could have worn to keep his core body temperature cool in case the Tour was as hot and humid as it had been the previous year. There was a helmet that had temperature sensors and would flood with chilly coolant, which would also lower Lance's core temperature. Theoretically, he would have been able to work harder (which generates more heat) because he would have stayed cooler. There were superporous one-piece skinsuits that shuttled away sweat like a fire hose. Superlight shoes. Other crazy gizmos. No matter how outlandish an idea seemed, if it was legal we at least considered it: there was the idea of a traveling bus that could be sealed tight and used as a mobile altitude chamber. (Sleeping in an altitude chamber—which replicates the low-oxygen conditions of living at high altitudes and helps the body adapt in a way that lets it carry and process more oxygen—is a staple of many top pros' training programs.) There was the idea of a time-trial bike that would have a bladder embedded in its tubes to hold water, eliminating the need for a water bottle. The million-dollar bike, though, that was real. It was no pipe dream, nor some mad-scientist concoction that would never leave the napkin it had been scrawled on. Lance was riding the bike, and we had objective proof that, at least when measured by a computer, it was faster than our old bike.

And we were going to discard it. We were going to ride the old bike.

I picked up the phone to begin making calls, to tell Trek and the rest of the F-One team that—though we appreciated all the work and all the money and all the time and resources and the startling innovations they'd brought to the world of cycling—we had to make our decision based on how Lance felt. I knew Lance and I were doing the right thing. But those calls were not going to be easy to make.

We'd used our heads—we'd studied the science of cycling technology with a depth and a scope no one had ever before brought to the sport. But, finally, I was going with my heart once again, just as I always had.

Before I made that first call, I sat for a long time, thinking about heart, belief, instinct.

In the 1998 Tour de France, I'd gotten caught up in a crash and broken two ribs. I was out of the Tour. I was thirty-four; the year before, I'd crashed and broken my pelvis. I wasn't tired of racing, but my body was.

As I sat there thinking about why we had to pull the plug on the F-One bike, I remembered how similarly clear and inevitable my decision to quit racing back in 1998 had seemed. I'd simply gone to my team director and said, "I'm done. I don't got it anymore. I stop." I'd had a contract until the end of the year, and I could have limped along, drawn my salary. But my heart was telling me no. I wasn't poor back then, but I definitely didn't have enough money to retire. I'd never ridden at a level, like Lance or even George Hincapie or Levi Leipheimer, that had earned me enough money to stop worrying about earning money. I'd been a worker in cycling, and I'd have to be a worker once I stopped racing. But that didn't seem to matter. I walked away from my contract, just like that—a racer one day, unemployed the next.

In the end, of course, that impulsive move to quit was what left me free to take up Lance's offer to run his team. Following my heart in a direction away from the guaranteed money of my contract changed my life. Gave me a chance to make my dreams come true. Gave me enough money to retire whenever I want. Gave me my friend, Lance Armstrong.

I picked up the phone and made the first call.

On that old bike, Lance won both time trials in his record-setting 2004 Tour de France, plus three other mountain stages, and finished the race 6:19 ahead of Andreas Klöden. Ullrich was nearly nine minutes behind. We also won the team time trial.

Even so, I consider the million dollars we spent on F-One to be a great investment. In the first place, just the mere existence of the F-One team had done us a lot of good. All of our rivals were aware that we were developing something amazing—we had let word leak that the wind tunnel tests showed that our bike was unmatched, but we never let out the news that Lance wasn't going to ride it. The threat of our new bike eroded their confidence in their own gear. Ullrich was quoted in the cycling press as saying, "I'm sure Lance has the fastest bike in the world."

Another thing F-One accomplished was to convince Lance that he could be dominant on the bikes we had. He received a huge psychological boost when we realized that he was faster on our old bike; he felt as if we'd gone as far technologically as we could, then picked the best solution.

The new bike didn't go completely to waste, either. Eki—Viatcheslav Ekimov—borrowed it and rode to a silver medal in the Olympic time trial.

But for me the real million-dollar payoff was the reminder that at the heart of winning lies heart. Technology can help you win. So can a team bus. A solid recruiting program. An inspiring mission statement. But none of those things actually do the winning. A million dollars can't ride a bicycle. Neither can a million bits of data. Races aren't contested in wind tunnels.

It's people who perform—out on roads and all across the world, whether their ambition is to win the Tour de France or open a restaurant or find a sponsor for the youth-league uniforms. And it's the people who have the heart to ignore the distractions—of money and technology and managers and everything else that clamors to be part of our lives—who win the most.

// WHAT I LEARNED FROM LOSING

10

"Lucky to Stare So Boldly at Loss"

*I had to not only accept the idea of losing, but find
ways to appreciate it—so I could learn from it as
much as I had from my victories.*

I WASN'T SHOCKED in April 2005 when Lance announced to the
world that the upcoming Tour de France would be his last, win
or lose. I hadn't even been surprised earlier that year when, in
private, he told me that he was planning to retire after July.

I was stunned, quite honestly, that he'd decided to race at all
that year.

It had become our tradition, beginning in 1999, the first season Lance and I won the Tour de France, to sit down within a few
weeks after the end of the race and start planning for the next one.
We never waited for the winter—the off-season—to discuss what
we thought our weakness had been, how we could improve on it,
what new thing we should try out. There was a very real practi-
cality to what we were doing; it was a way to make sure we stayed
ahead of the competition. But it was also a deliberately symbolic
gesture, an important ritual we each appreciated: it reminded us
that one of the foundations of our success was that we were simply willing to outwork all our rivals—to start sooner, work harder,
focus more intensely, and devote ourselves fully to victory.

When he and I sat down in 2004, we hadn't yet even reached

the point where we were ready to discuss strategy, or training, or teammates or rivals or rumors about the course of the 2005 Tour (which wasn't released yet). No—we were trying to decide if there would *be* a 2005 Tour for Lance.

For years, both of us had operated on the assumption, without making a big deal out of it in public, that seven Tour victories was the magic number. In fact, way back in 2003, before Lance had won even his fifth Tour, we were sitting together in his hotel room at the Tour of Murcia. It was only his first or second race of that season, and we were reviewing how we wanted the year to unfold. I glanced over at the screensaver on his laptop computer, and the word "Courage," in bright yellow, caught my eye.

But I looked again; something wasn't quite right. The word was spelled COU2AGE.

I really looked at the screen now. There were seven words on it, in a column, all in yellow:

HOPE
COU2AGE
PERS3VERANCE
WIS4OM
INTE5RITY
DE6TINY
MAG7C

Someone at Nike had created it for Lance—three full years before he won his seventh Tour, back at a time when the thought of just five victories in Paris seemed outrageous to most of the public, and to a good part of the pro peloton.

We'd always had that magic number, seven, in mind. But in 2004, unexpectedly, we had both experienced a letdown after his last triumph, number six. Neither of us ever thought of ourselves as athletes who were driven by the thought of setting records. We raced to win, not to set records. It really was as simple as that: we loved to win. But since Lance had stood atop the podium that July for the sixth consecutive time, both of us had also admitted to each other that his victory—which put him one above any of the other great champions: Indurain, Hinault, Merckx, Anquetil —had ended up meaning much more to us than we'd anticipated. Consciously or not, I realized, in some way we'd been driving for some time toward that unprecedented, record-setting, sixth Tour de France.

With the record broken, with Lance standing alone atop the list of multiple-Tour winners, that unspoken motivation was gone. What could the Tour offer us now?

Lance didn't need its winnings; he was wealthy from past wins, sponsorships, smart investments from his youth, and his skill in the stock market. Fame? Thanks to his activism with cancer survivorship, he was already a bigger worldwide celebrity than any winner of any bike race could ever hope to be. Plus, his involvement in the fight against cancer gave him a deeper, richer satisfaction than cycling could; the Tour de France, as I like to say, is a metaphor for life. The fight against cancer *is* life.

In terms of sporting challenge, there was little left. Lance had not only won six Tours, but six in a row against a changing cast of opponents—he was no fluke, no lucky winner with something left to prove to his colleagues and rivals.

He and I were also deeply unsettled and disturbed by a dark turn the sport had taken. Remember that we were talking in August 2004, so some of the highest-profile doping scandals had yet to hit: there would be the September 2004 announcement that Tyler Hamilton might have failed two blood-doping tests (one was at the Athens Olympics earlier that year—which was later nullified because a second sample, known as a "B" sample, and required to prove guilt, had been damaged by the testing lab—and one was later at the Vuelta a España); there would be the positive test for the hormone erythropoietin (EPO) that would cost our former teammate Roberto Heras (who was riding for a different team by then) his Tour of Spain crown in 2005; there would be the 2006 Operación Puerto criminal investigation, which alleged that numerous racers were corroborating with a Spanish doctor to dope, and which would end up keeping superstars such as Jan Ullrich, Ivan Basso, and seven other racers from competing in the 2006 Tour de France; there would be the positive testosterone result attributed to Floyd Landis during stage 17 of the 2006 Tour de France (when, in an epic mountain stage, he took back the yellow jersey); and, topping everything, there would be the meltdown of the 2007 Tour de France, in which the entire Cofidis team pulled out of the race after their rider Christian Moreni tested positive for testosterone, the Astana team withdrew after its team leader and double stage winner Alexander Vinokourov returned a positive sample for blood doping, Patrik Sinkewitz was kicked out after it was confirmed that he failed a test for testosterone doping before the Tour, Iban Mayo's "A" sample, tested on a rest day, indicated EPO use, and Michael Rasmussen was withdrawn from the race and fired by his team—while wearing yellow—for violating team policy by not accurately reporting his whereabouts to cycling's dope-testing agencies in the month before the Tour. (A pro racer must be available at all times for what's known as out-of-competition testing.)

I'm fond of telling people—perhaps overly so—that the Tour de France is a metaphor for life. And, like life, the Tour has always brought out the worst as well as the best in humankind. From its beginning, the Tour has been a showcase for dishonesty, chaos, and cheating right alongside virtues such as nobility, bravery, sacrifice, and triumph. In 1904, the second Tour de France ever, the top four riders were disqualified for taking a train during key stages—and twenty-five other riders out of the field of eighty-eight were punished for riding in cars or trains when they should have been on their bikes, or for taking shortcuts. The next year, fans of François Dortignacq covered the road with nails and tacks in stage 1, giving all his rivals flat tires. In 1911 the brothers Henri and Francis Pélissier pulled out a flask and showed it to journalist Albert Londres, telling him it was a cocaine mixture. "We keep going on dynamite," Henri told the reporter. "In the evenings, we dance around our rooms instead of sleeping." In 1937, just before starting a mountain stage, eventual winner Roger Lapébie noticed that his handlebar had been partially sawn through in an act of sabotage. In 1953 a superlean, tiny climber named Jean Robic would secretly take a water bottle filled with lead (weighing about twenty-five pounds) at the crest of climbs so he could descend faster.

The methods of cheating in the Tour had begun with roguish stunts such as hopping onto trains and throwing tacks. But now it had gone all the way to sophisticated medical procedures. The atmosphere of cycling felt more poisonous than ever—even amid the inspirational, beautiful triumph of a man surviving cancer and going on to become the greatest champion of the greatest sporting event. The pervasive problem of doping was turning many reporters, fans—and sometimes even the racers themselves—into skeptics: Could they believe what they were seeing? Since he'd won his first Tour in 1999, Lance had been dogged by suspicion, innuendo, and outright, but always unfounded, accusations that he'd doped. The media dug through our team's trash, looking for evidence of cheating. Riders from other teams accused him of doping, and sometimes so did former staff members and racers who'd left the team (some of them after being paid for their stories by reporters)—but none of them could ever show a shred of proof that backed up what they claimed. From 1999 to his retirement in 2005, Lance was the most tested athlete on the planet; he had never failed a single in- or out-of-competition drug test. Yet because of rumor and accusation we often felt as if he'd been put in the impossible situation of having to come up with tangible proof that he had nothing to prove—what evidence could we offer that he didn't dope, aside from his record of spotless tests?

Imagine that, in the absence of a body or any other evidence or factual proof of a crime, and despite the lack of official charges by the police or prosecutor, your neighbor suddenly accused you of murder one day—and the local papers and television stations blared the news as if it were true. How would you feel? What proof could you offer beyond the lack of proof?

It was in this atmosphere in 2004 that Lance and I were dis-

cussing whether he should try for a seventh win the following year
— no more records to be won, no more significant financial, sporting, or humanitarian advantages, and the ongoing, maddening circumstance of trying again and again to prove our innocence and
defend ourselves against accusations without proof.

On the other hand, if we committed to another Tour we knew
that we had to offer almost everything. Directing the team had become an occupation that consumed me, no less than him. Training for the Tour — the way we did it — was a year-round, day-long
occupation that dictated his diet, his sleep, his vacations, his social habits ranging from how much TV he got to watch to which
friends he ended up seeing, and, most important to Lance, how
much time he could spend with his son and twin daughters.

"So," I said to him, "if we would go for seven what would be the
reason? Why?"

He grinned and said, "To win."

I smiled back at him. He was already gaining back some of the
weight he'd lost during the Tour de France. By the last day, a Tour
rider looks gaunt, sick, starved. There was color in Lance's skin,
and a certain springiness to his motions again. His eyes burned
with intensity.

"Yes," I said. "But should we?"

It turned out to be an interesting question. Without stopping to
censor ourselves, the two of us ticked off a long, improvised list of
things that would motivate us, ideals that made winning another
Tour worthwhile, ranging from serious topics such as "continuing
exposure for the cancer survivorship program" to business goals
such as "seven will help us secure sponsorships" to ancillary ideas
such as "seven might put the record out of reach" to the down-
right silly — "let's show them an old man can still win one." (Lance
would be approaching thirty-four in the 2005 Tour; his birthday is
in September.)

It was one of the most honest conversations I'd ever had in my
life, because neither of us had a predetermined outcome in mind;
each of us was willing to accept a yes or a no as the right answer.

Oddly, I wasn't scared or even nervous about the thought of not being able to count on Lance in the Tour. And I even felt free to bring that up.

"You know," I said, "I have to win at least one Tour without you."

We both knew why: to consider myself a winner—not just someone who'd won a lot, but someone who was, in a fundamental and unchangeable way, a winner inside and to the core—I had to show myself and the world that I could direct a team to at least one more win without the world's greatest cyclist turning the pedals for me. If I didn't, I'd spend the rest of my life wondering if I was as good as I'd thought.

"Johan," Lance said in that way of his that suggested there was only one choice. "You will."

I thought back to one night I'd spent somewhere in a hotel room on yet one more road trip after Lance had won his fourth Tour back in 2002. I remember sitting alone for hours, forcing myself to really think about my next step after Lance retired. The idea had passed through my thoughts now and then, but only in the way the risk of a bicycle crash does: you know it will happen *someday,* and that someday could be any day—but almost certainly won't be today. It was always easier to not think about the end of our streak than to plan for what would come afterward.

I'm not sure what event finally convinced me to stop ignoring the subject during that night I spent alone deep in thought in 2002. I only know that I did it just in time. What I mean is, if I hadn't started focusing on the problem so early—three full cycling seasons before Lance retired—there's a good chance that after we won our last Tour together in 2005 I would have drifted aimlessly, like a boat accidentally loosed from its mooring. I needed all that time to really, and fully, accept a cold reality: even though I believed I could win the Tour again without Lance, I felt certain that I would lose at least once without him, because when I won again it would have to be with a very different kind of team and a very different kind of rider—which meant that I would have to be very different, too. All of that reimagining would take time, certainly at least one season and perhaps many, many more.

In one very important way, I was lucky to stare so boldly at loss. Coaches, managers, even entire sports leagues sometimes spend years and years searching fruitlessly for a way to return to a time of unmatchable glory. The best modern example: the fans, media, and officials of the NBA never seemed to be able to stop yearning for "the next Michael Jordan." I knew without a doubt there was no "next Lance Armstrong." I'd been close witness to too many miraculous physical feats, too many unprecedented instances of courage, intensity, focus. I'd studied too many numbers—wattage outputs and heart rates and oxygen-uptake measurements and power-to-weight ratios, and on and on. Most of all: I'd spent literally countless hours riding in a car behind and beside Lance Armstrong.

There was not going to be a next Lance Armstrong.

But there was going to be a next—and I did not want to fail when it came.

In the end, I still can't point to one factor that led Lance and me to try that one more Tour together in 2005. Maybe it was a mix of all the reasons—just because we could, just to show everyone we could, because we were not ready to stop winning yet, because one more year with Lance would buy us one more year to try to find his heir and reshape our team, for the money, for the fame, for the satisfaction. Maybe it all came down to that word on the screensaver, MAG7C. The fact that neither of us can cite one overwhelming reason Lance decided to race again in 2005 makes me think that, in the end, we staked our pride one more time to that legendary, simple phrase we'd latched on to so long ago: "We might as well win."

There's a joke in cycling: 50 percent of winning is just showing up.

The remaining 50 percent is crossing the finish line first.

It's funny—unless you're a team director contemplating how to win a Tour de France without Lance Armstrong.

Then the joke gets a little more personal. It goes like this: Seven-eighths of being a winner is showing up with Lance Armstrong. The remaining one-eighth is simply gathering everything I ever learned about the Tour de France on my own and with Lance and the rest of the team — years and years of hard-won wisdom about strength and strategy and discipline and obsessive attention to the smallest details and sacrifice and sweat and how you have to be willing to risk all that work in the one key moment when the race hangs in the balance. Then I would have to use that knowledge like a hammer and, against the anvil of the greatest, cruelest, most beautiful and terrible sporting event in the world, forge a way to win that was entirely new.

Life with Lance had taught me a lot about how to win — start with belief, use your head and your heart, communicate, don't be afraid to dent things, confide, hide your strengths, lose a little to win a lot, never stop seeking talent to surround yourself with, and don't let money make your most important decisions for you. But before I could truly become a winner in my own eyes, I had to figure out a way to triumph in the Tour without Lance. And to do that, I had to accomplish something that goes against my nature. I had to not only accept the idea of losing, but find ways to appreciate it — so I could learn from it as much as I had from my victories.

11

When Failure Is Inevitable, Limit the Damage

*Avoiding the complete loss of all you've worked for
can be a sweet victory amid even the cruelest defeat.*

THERE ARE ALL THESE little sayings in cycling: Eat before
you're hungry, drink before you're thirsty. Shift before a climb.
Brake before a turn. It's easier to ride at the front than the
back. Pedal circles.

These nuggets of wisdom don't sound all that brilliant, I know.
In fact, if anything they sound too simple — but I'm pretty sure
that's why they're so useful. During the rigor of a race, it's hard to
think. In fact, I'd say that one of the reasons I've been so successful
as a team director is not solely — or maybe even mainly — because
of our innovations or because our race strategies are brilliant. It's
just that, amid the chaos of a bike race, I'm able to get our team
to execute the simple, basic moves that are the foundation of the
sport. And all those fundamental, strong phrases that remind you
of the right things to do can make a big difference.

In the 2000 Tour de France, one of these sayings saved our
whole race.

Lance and I knew that winning his second yellow jersey in 2000
would be tougher than the first, because two of the best racers

—both former champions of the Tour de France—hadn't competed in 1999. Jan Ullrich, our perpetual nemesis and the Tour winner in 1997, had been off his bike due to nagging injuries through much of 1999. Marco Pantani, a climbing sensation who'd won the yellow jersey in 1998 and who was as erratic and unpredictable as he was gifted, had returned to the sport after being embroiled in a doping scandal.

There were three big, important mountaintop finishes in the 2000 Tour, and we knew that Ullrich and Pantani knew the same thing we did: that's where the race would be won and lost.

The first mountain stage was about 130 miles and climbed over two large peaks before ending on Hautacam, a monster that climbed nearly eight and a half miles at about an 8 percent grade. We'd ridden it a lot in training that spring—with good and bad results. Early in May, Lance was descending on its narrow roads after a practice climb when his tire suddenly exploded and he veered right into a brick wall. He got banged up and bruised, and missed a couple weeks of training. In June, we went back to ride it again—and that was the famously cold, bitter, rain-lashed day when Lance got to the top and said to me, "Let's do it again."

When the Hautacam stage came in the Tour, Lance was in sixteenth place overall, nearly six minutes behind the leader. That was okay: the race had so far covered only the flat and rolling stages ruled by sprinters and breakaway specialists, the guys whose ambition was only to wear the yellow jersey for a few days rather than at the end. Our key rivals were behind us, including Ullrich, who was about half a minute farther back, and Pantani, who was more than eleven minutes behind the top spot.

We woke in the morning to the sound of rain battering the windows of our hotel. The streets looked cold, drenched, miserable—perfect for us. Lance had trained on Hautacam in identical weather. He greeted me with a huge smile, and said, "Good day for a bike race."

It would turn out to be more than a good day.

As the pack splashed along tiny French roads, three riders took off on an early attack. We let them go, because none were threats to our overall victory.

"Lose the stage, win the jersey," I said over the radio, putting one of those race homilies into the riders' heads for reassurance.

The shivering pack—and the suffering breakaway group—was reduced to tatters by the storm. Eventually only a young racer named Javier Otxoa was left out in front of us. A group of five or so climbers, about eight minutes back, was chasing him to the foot of Hautacam. We'd let them get away, as well. I'd only cared about getting Lance into a second big group that was nearly eleven minutes behind Otxoa, but contained our main rivals. The rest of the peloton was scattered across the windswept roads.

As the road tipped skyward, Pantani rose out of his saddle and attacked, leaping forward out of the big group. Lance followed, then blew by him, furiously spinning his pedals yet looking as smooth as if he were out on a Sunday afternoon jaunt through the countryside. He caught the group chasing Otxoa and went through them like a bowling ball through the pins.

A sole racer remained in front of us, and though Lance ate up the gap between them like a ravenous man—making up ten minutes in a mere eight miles—Otxoa hung on to win by forty-one seconds.

We didn't care. Lance had taken over the yellow jersey and put time between himself and Ullrich (who was now 4:14 back) as well as Pantani (who was 10:34 behind Lance).

After a smaller climbing day, we came to the next key mountain stage: Ventoux. This thirteen-mile climb, called the Giant of Provence because it towers isolated and monolithic over the surrounding region, is relentlessly steep and unforgiving. It peaks at over sixty-two hundred feet, so high the thin air burns as it enters your lungs, and winds constantly whip its exposed, treeless, lunarlike final miles. At the foot of Ventoux, I sent our two best climbers to the front with another one of those one-sentence directives that meant so much: "Drop the hammer." That meant their job was to smash the pack apart—and within a few miles they had exhausted themselves and, as directed, shattered the race. It was just what I'd wanted: only Lance, Ullrich, Pantani, and three other climbers remained at the front. Now that we were in yellow, all we had to do was make sure Lance could follow his closest rivals. We no longer needed to attack; we needed only to preserve our advantage, not gain one.

Ullrich was pushing the pace in his characteristic way, sitting and grinding at the pedals, the big muscles of his legs looking like some kind of machinery. Pantani kept losing contact with the group—falling behind, then battling his way back onto the tail before faltering. He seemed to be fighting a fierce war within his own body. He fell back once more, and I said "Sitting good" to Lance over our radios.

Out of nowhere, Pantani rushed up through the group and jumped off the front. The tiny pack bobbed and clawed its way up to him, and just as it did he jumped again. Someone fell off the back—I never noticed who; I was busy watching Lance to make sure he had the strength to cover these withering assaults. Pantani jumped again, and again, each time shedding more riders from the group. Something about the tiny pack—maybe the growing space between the riders, or the way some of their shoulders were bobbing—told me that Pantani's next attack was going to completely crack the group. I grabbed for the radio and said, "Go with him this time!"

When Pantani attacked, Lance spun up to him, then did something remarkable. Rather than sitting on Pantani's wheel, using it as a mental carrot to pace himself and as a slight shield from the 40-mph winds that were battering them, Lance rode up beside Pantani and they pedaled two wide up the road as steep as a wall.

That's when the trouble started.

When the wearer of the yellow jersey escapes with a rider who is no threat to his lead, it is customary—and considered honorable—to grant the stage win to the other rider. The most important goal for the leader is to gain time on his rivals, so when a rider helps him do that, giving up the stage win is a way of saying thanks. It's one of the traditions of racing. So at the top, Lance eased up on his pedals to let Pantani cross the line first.

It's hard to say exactly what went wrong. Pantani was a proud, volatile racer, and it could be that he was stung by Lance's gift —knowing it meant, in essence, that Lance no longer considered him a threat for the overall win. Lance also says that, while the two of them rode alone toward the peak, he tried to say "Victory" in Italian as a crude way of telling Pantani he could win the stage—but Pantani thought he heard the word *vitesse,* which means "faster" and could have been interpreted as a taunt. Whatever happened, Lance's gift blew up in our faces. At the press conference afterward, Pantani vowed to tear apart the race.

It was not an idle threat. The next day, on one of the minor mountain stages, the Italian rode away from the pack, finishing fifty seconds ahead of Lance, then saying at a press conference: "It's much more satisfying to finish alone," as if it was only for the lack of thinking of it that he hadn't won solo the day before.

The last big mountain stage of the 2000 Tour de France became what Lance would later tell me was "the hardest day of my life—on a bike."

Stage 16 packed five climbs into eighty-four miles of racing. The last ascent was called the Joux-Plane, a seven-and-a-half mile terror steeper than Ventoux or Hautacam, with twisty, narrow Alpine roads that lay across the mountain as if they'd been thrown there by a careless giant.

Pantani attacked on the very first climb of the day—a madman's tactic, an insane gamble that he could dance over the final four mountains and seventy-five miles by himself. There was almost no chance he could succeed.

But there was a chance.

Because of his earlier victory, I had to take his attack seriously. He was blasting away from the pack, his pink jersey bobbing as he stood and slapped his pedals up and down in that distinctive gait he had. Pantani had shaved his head, wore a goatee, earring, and bandanna, and had christened himself Il Pirata, the pirate. It was more likely than not that he was going to do nothing more than sink his own ship, but I couldn't take the chance that he might steal our Tour de France.

"Okay, boys," I radioed to the team. "Let's do a little chasing."

I kept my voice calm, nearly laconic. I wanted the team to think this was nothing more than another routine defense of the yellow jersey. I also wanted to defuse some of the tension that everyone had felt building around Lance and Pantani. And, riding in the car with me that day was a VIP guest, the prime minister of Belgium, my homeland. I smiled at him and said, "This will be fun now, to watch." Two of our best climbers went to the front of the group and began hauling the pack behind them as if they were Alaskan sled dogs.

Pantani's lead grew to a full minute.

"More gas," I said, striving for an intense lightness of tone. "Bring him back. Now." The prime minister raised his eyebrows. I nodded my head, though I was not sure why.

Our team chased the Italian over two more climbs, heads down, pushing hard, and so intent on the pursuit that some of them sped right through the feed zone, not wanting to waste even a second slowing down to grab a musette bag full of food. Our doggedness paid off: though at one point Pantani's lead stretched out to 1:05, on a descent before Joux-Plane we came rushing around him like a wave engulfing a child. Pantani's pink jersey and bandanna became lost amid all the colors of the jerseys in the pack.

Now it was up to Lance. Within a few pedal strokes he left the ragged pack and began climbing the Joux-Plane with just three other riders: Ullrich, the French climbing star Richard Virenque, and a climbing specialist from Spain.

This was more like it.

"Johan." It was Lance.

I swept the handpiece up toward my mouth with a jaunty flourish, tipping my head at the prime minister. "What is it, Lance?"

"I'm not feeling great."

"You're good," I said. "Ten k to the summit."

But he was not good. For the first time in two years, Lance's legs faltered. His shoulders hunched. And his bike slowed.

Ullrich, who was just maintaining the pace, opened a gap. Virenque followed him. Then they both realized what had happened, and they actually turned their heads and looked at Lance, as if they needed proof.

"Don't worry, Lance," I said. "We're okay. We're okay. This is okay."

But inside my head, my brain was spinning as frantically as a cyclist's legs during an attack. I knew Lance's fitness level. We'd trained on these climbs. We'd done more climbing on those early spring days than we faced in the real Tour stages. He couldn't be cracking. Or could he? Had Pantani really done it—blown up the race?

"You're good, Lance," I said, and turned my head and smiled again at the prime minister.

Out on the road, Ullrich began to grind away at a huge gear, flooding his bike with his mighty wattage, and beside him Virenque and the other climber began that fluttering, dancing motion the tiny ascenders make as they attack.

Lance's head began bobbing, as if he were trying to pedal his bike with every part of his body. His voice, again: "Johan?"

If Lance was falling apart, our Tour was over. Our streak would end at exactly one.

"Johan?" he said.

I clicked the talk button on the mike, then let it off. Ullrich's group was disappearing up the Joux-Plane. I played the entire stage over in my head again—and I knew what had gone wrong. In the heat of the chase, Lance had skipped the feed zone along with some of the other riders on our team. And now we were paying for it. On the narrow road, there was no way to get food or water up to him.

One of the most frustrating aspects of being a team director is when the race is suddenly out of your hands—when the fundamentals simply aren't executed by the riders on the road. No strategy, no brilliance, no motivation, no inspiration, no alternate plans—nothing matters if the riders fail to execute what you tell them. The magic between Lance and me was that such breakdowns never happened. We had raced like one being—a brain in the car and a body on the bike. Until now.

We had just failed to execute.

And we had failed in a way that could cost us the Tour de France. If a rider completely bonks—totally runs out of energy and hydration—it's like a car losing gas and oil all at once. Everything shuts down disastrously. You don't just stop; the engine seizes.

When you suffer such a fundamental failure, only a fundamental solution can save the day. I knew that only one thing could win the Tour de France for us now, a four-word phrase so basic a second-grader could have uttered it.

"Lance," I said into the radio, "ride within your limits."

I turned to the prime minister and smiled again, and this time it was a sincere gesture, not a camouflage. I said, "This is pretty bad. But it's under control now."

Lance was in no condition to either stage a counterattack or even try to chase Ullrich and Virenque. The only way he'd survive the stage was backing off to a level of intensity that would let him crawl his way to the finish—just fast enough to preserve his body and our lead. It was counterintuitive, but even though we were losing ground, we had to actually slow down—avoid blowing the engine while finding the pace that was just enough to keep us in yellow. As I was thinking all of this out, another part of my brain was doing some math: mileage left versus how much time he had on Ullrich at the start of the stage, versus the climbing speed I estimated for each rider.

I brought the radio up and said, "Lance, listen. You have a big lead. You can afford to give two minutes back. You can afford three minutes. Slow down."

I repeated the simple, race-saving wisdom: "Ride within your limits."

And that's what he did. By no means was it easy. At one point, as I kept up my ongoing string of soothing encouragement, he didn't answer me for minutes. When he finally spoke, his voice sounded shaky, hollow.

But he rode within his limits. He crawled up that mountain at a pace that would have embarrassed him just the day before. Just the hour before. But now his progress was a testament of willpower and strength. And savvy.

When a loss is inevitable, sometimes you shouldn't waste your energy or time fighting in vain. Better to accept an unavoidable loss and figure out a way to limit its consequences. Avoiding the complete loss of all you've worked for can be a sweet victory amid even the cruelest defeat. Had Lance pushed his failing body beyond its limits on this stage, the entire Tour de France very well might have slipped away from us.

Virenque won the stage that day. Ullrich finished second, and in the end gained only ninety-seven seconds on Lance, still leaving us with a cushion of more than five and a half minutes. Pantani fell apart and lost thirteen minutes. The next day, he dropped out of the Tour de France.

12

Find a Victory in Every Loss

Sometimes if you stare long enough at a loss without blinking, you see an edge that you might have missed if you merely excused your failure and moved on.

GEORGE HINCAPIE is a tall, lean, stylish cyclist who is not only one of Lance's best friends, but the only racer in the world who rode with Lance for all seven Tour de France victories. He's kind of a cross between Frank Sinatra, Paul Newman, and George Clooney, if they were combined into a single world-class cyclist. At six foot three, he's tall for a cyclist, but with a racing weight around 170–175 pounds he strikes a whiplike figure —think the elegant power of a greyhound. He seemed to have the most natural ability as a sprinter when he began cycling, but in the process of becoming Lance's most trusted lieutenant, George trained himself to be able to pull the pack along for half a day, or lead Lance high up into the mountains. He'd ride his heart out for his friend—and often did. Yet he's no second banana—he's a worldwide star in his own right, a top racer who's good-looking, suave, and erudite enough to have romanced and married Melanie Simonneau, a former podium girl (one of the dazzling women who each day present flowers, jerseys, and trophies to the stage's winners) with whom he has a daughter, Julia Paris. George also designed his own line of Euro-inspired, vintage-look-but-high-tech bike wear. I guess if you didn't think it sounded too corny, you could without reservation call him a renaissance man.

I always wanted to win Paris-Roubaix—the Classic known as the Hell of the North—with George. He's the best one-day rider the United States has ever produced, especially when it comes to those hard, gritty, early-season races contested all across Europe. Though you wouldn't know it from reading the sports pages in America, the cyclists hardy enough, smart enough, and lucky enough to win a Classic are revered as champions. George is the only American to win Ghent-Wevelgem, one of the jewels of the Classics, and another well-respected race, Kuurne-Brussels-Kuurne. How to explain it? If the Tour de France is like winning an Oscar, a Classic is like the Palm d'Or at Cannes or the top prize at the Sundance festival.

Probably the best known of the Classics is Paris-Roubaix. Imagine a race that for 160 miles splatters riders across mud fields, jackhammers their bodies bloody on ragged cobblestone paths from another century, pitches them into gutters, and runs them through a gauntlet of drunken, screaming fanatics—before finishing incongruously with one and a half laps on a gleaming oval velodrome. The race is considered by many to be the hardest and greatest one-day race in the world. No American racer has ever come close to winning it.

Except George.

In 1999, with only about 15 miles to go (after more than 140 miles of racing), he was in a lead group of seven when the Italian champion Andrea Tafi attacked—while two of his teammates went to the front of the narrow cobbled road and blocked everyone from chasing. Tafi stayed away to win; George finished fourth, just one step off the podium.

In 2000, George and a small group of chasers tried to defy destiny: Johan Museeuw, considered one of the greatest Classics racers ever, had returned to Paris-Roubaix for redemption two years after a crash on its cobbles nearly caused him to lose his leg to gangrene. Museeuw had attacked and, with only 18 of the 170 miles to go, held a lead of nearly three minutes. George and his chasing group began a desperate effort that ate away huge chunks of the lead—less than two minutes with 10 miles to go, less than a minute with about 2 miles to the finish, half a minute at half a mile, and finally, at the finish, the charging group was a mere fifteen seconds behind. George was sixth.

In 2001, after rainstorms so fierce that local fire departments had to be called in to pump water off the cobbled course — making for a gooey, pasty race that the organizers called the worst conditions they'd ever seen — George had escaped alone with 50 miles to go, then punctured a tire, was caught by a chasing group, and finished fourth. And so it went: sixth in 2002 after slipping in the mud and riding into a ditch, kept out of the race in 2003 by a respiratory and parasitic infection, and eighth in 2004 — capping a remarkable run of top ten placings in a race that routinely ends careers with its bone-snapping crashes and matter-of-factly breaks hearts that reside in strong bodies rendered weak by punctured tires, smashed wheels, and busted frames. Paris-Roubaix is a race of agonizingly small differences; in 1990 Steve Bauer lost his bid at legendary status by *one centimeter* to Eddy Planckaert.

To me, George has been so close to winning Paris-Roubaix so many times that he is one of those riders whose destiny and the race's seem intertwined. I had a gut feeling that 2005 was going to be his year.

We'd stacked the team with riders we knew could support George in wretched conditions: two hard-nosed Belgians, Stijn Devolder and Leif Hoste; a former mountain biker, Ryder Hesjedal, who'd won seven world-championship medals off-road; Roger Hammond, a Brit who could go to the front of any pack and drive the pace like a locomotive; and the indomitable Eki — Viatcheslav Ekimov — who was by then considered the grandmaster of all cycling. And the conditions were nightmarish. The race began in hot, sunny weather that covered the riders with dust, which commingled with sweat then baked to a hard crust on their bodies. The pace was blistering, and crashes were slicing apart the pack every time the riders entered a tough section of cobbles. Ludo Dierckxsens, a wily veteran racer, crashed into barbed wire. Frédéric Guesdon, the 1997 winner, crashed and destroyed his bike.

In Paris-Roubaix, there's not much of a strategy beyond imploring your support riders to be near your captain. The lanes are barely narrow enough to fit the team cars, and so clogged with riders that passing is nearly impossible. We screamed at our riders to find George, to lead him to the best lines over the ragged roads — screamed because otherwise they wouldn't have been able to hear us over the pandemonium of the crowds. Spectators from all over Europe come to Paris-Roubaix and line the roads ten deep, but the most rabid fans are the Belgians, who camp out along the course and prepare for the spectacle by drinking beer and eating *frites* — French fries — for hours. I've always thought that riding on cobbles through a crowd of flag-waving Belgians must be like being a Marine recruit at boot camp: madness. George loves it.

It began raining. On the slickened cobbles, the carnage was indescribable. Peter Van Petegem, the 2003 winner, crashed and broke his hip. George flatted, one of our support cars screeched to a halt, skidding to a stop just inches from him as the mechanic shot out and replaced the wheel in less than five seconds then frantically pushed him, slipping and sliding in the growing mud. Another racer, Sébastien Chavanel, crashed, got up quickly, and called for a new bike from one of the neutral support vehicles that follow the racers. As Chavanel remounted and sped away, the car had to accelerate to stay in front of the hard-charging pack; it bounced over the cobblestones like a soccer ball, sliding and careening the width of the narrow lane — as a mechanic stood on the roof, desperately holding on to the bike rack for life.

Through the cobbles, George outrode everyone but Juan Antonio Flecha and a Belgian racer, Tom Boonen, who'd already won the Tour of Flanders that year and would go on to become the world champion at the end of the season. Boonen was having a career year. He was the man to beat.

After six and a half hours of racing during which the leaders felt as if they were being beaten in the back by a baseball bat, the three riders rode into the parking lot of the velodrome in Paris. Even from the outside, they could hear the roar of the cheering fans packing the stadium. No American had ever been this close, this far.

George was at the front when they entered the velodrome — not the place to be. If he jumped for the finish, the other two would sit in his draft then sweep around him at the last minute. George eased off the pedals — could he force someone else to go to the front? There was nothing any coach could tell him now.

As quick as an eye blink, Flecha attacked, hoping he could surge away on a wave of surprise. George caught his wheel, sat in the draft, and readied to sprint. But meanwhile, Boonen had ridden high up on the banked turn of the velodrome, and using his down-hill momentum to power his bike, he swept by the other two, blurring his feet as he passed.

George leapt for Boonen's wheel, caught it — desperately clawed his way around and began inching forward as the line shot toward them. After years of close calls and bad luck, this was George's shot, his chance to be in the velodrome as the race was decided, maybe his only chance ever. I knew he would not waste it. He didn't. He poured everything he had into the pedals, everything he was.

Boonen won.

Afterward, in tears, George told me, "It was the best I had. I could not beat Boonen today. I couldn't do any more. I couldn't do any more. I did everything I could."

I knew he had — not just in the velodrome but throughout the race, coming back from the flat, avoiding the crashes, making the breakaways, chasing down the escapes. It was a mistake-free ride on a course that had pulverized the legends of the sport, ending in the narrowest of losses to a champion having the season of his life. Only 80 racers even made it to the velodrome, out of the 161 that started. It was the best finish ever by an American, the only po-dium finish ever by an American.

I reached out and hugged George, squeezing him tightly, lifting him off his feet, and I said, "Heroic."

And I meant it. I kept meaning it while I stood in the infield of the velodrome and watched George climb to the second-highest step of the podium. In Boonen's arms was the Paris-Roubaix trophy: a heavy, soccer-ball-size cobblestone taken from the legendary roads. In George's arms: his infant daughter, Julia Paris.

Sometimes the curtains of a loss part and you discover a hero, as both I and Julia Paris did on that day in the velodrome. And sometimes if you stare long enough at a loss without blinking, you see an edge that you might have missed if you merely excused your failure and moved on.

The 2003 Tour de France was the one that would put Lance in the company of the sport's legends—Anquetil, Merckx, Hinault, and Indurain, the only men in history who had won the race five times. It seemed as if legend itself was conspiring against us.

In the winter before the Tour, Lance separated from his wife. He doggedly stuck to his training through the emotional turmoil, but I could see that the upheaval was sapping some of his mental strength. Then he crashed in an early-season race we were using to warm up for the Tour, the Dauphiné Libéré. He developed tendonitis. A few weeks before the start of the Tour, while spending as much time with his kids as he could before the long period away from them, he picked up some illness or virus from one of them and got horribly sick.

Throughout that winter and spring Lance and I talked at least once a day, as we always did. Physically, he was about right where we needed him to be—we built our shared faith on that foundation, and I busied myself preparing a team that would be our best ever, that could buttress us against more bad luck and ill fate. By the time July came and the Tour de France began, we felt confident once more.

Lance finished seventh in the prologue.

Worse, our longtime rival (and most-feared competitor), Jan Ullrich, was looking fitter than he had back in 2001, when he'd given us so much trouble. He was surrounded by a new team, Bianchi, that had been assembled solely to support his run at this year's Tour de France.

Things didn't improve much. In the first stage, Lance got caught up in a big crash. He escaped with bumps, scrapes, and bruises, none of which were major but all of which added to the overall dragging effect we felt. The French sun burned down on the riders' backs, roasting the pack in its one-hundred-degree heat day after day. Lance was suffering.

But we did have a strong team—and by winning the team time trial we vaulted Lance from twelfth overall to second. (The only rider ahead of him, in fact, was our own Victor Hugo Peña, the climber who'd done so much good work for us in the past and who we were counting on for support again this year. We all, especially Lance, were happy to see Victor, the kind of under-the-headlines hard worker who rarely gets worldwide recognition, get his day in yellow.)

Still, bad luck—and disappointing results—plagued us. In a stage in the Alps, Lance rode most of the day—including an eighteen-mile climb up the massive Col du Galibier—with his back brake misadjusted and rubbing the pad, sapping his strength and costing us time. And when we got to Alpe d'Huez, weary from a year of struggle, Lance rode it from top to bottom four minutes slower than he had in 2001.

By the time we got to the individual time trial, Lance was in yellow but it had never felt less secure. There wasn't anything wrong with Lance—no physical malady, no plunge in the important numbers we monitored to gauge his fitness and power, no change in the mental toughness and focus he'd always had. It just seemed that our best suddenly wasn't good enough.

The time trial was twenty-nine miles; each person rode alone, against the clock, with no teammates for shelter and support, no pack to pace off. It was hot, dusty, windy. And Ullrich won by one minute, thirty-six seconds.

At the finish, Lance collapsed over his bike, then into the arms of our *soigneurs.* There was a pasty, white ring of salt around his mouth, and his body was crusty with dried salt and other minerals that had leeched out of his body. He looked drawn, as if he'd

shed his muscle somewhere on the course and was now just a skel-
eton of who he'd been. And, indeed, when he stepped on a scale
after the race, we found out he'd lost fifteen pounds during those
twenty-nine miles—nearly every bit of it fluid.

He'd dehydrated out there. He'd almost put himself into a
coma.

Whenever someone has a bad day, I try to find something positive to say before dinner. I analyze the race, and the performances,
and pick out some nugget we can focus on, some bit of information that seems to be a bright point in even the darkest moment.
The time trial ended at 5:30, so I immediately sequestered myself
and studied the time splits. I had to find an answer. I had to find
the way out of this dark tunnel we'd ridden into.

And there it was: In the first nine miles of the race, Lance had
ridden just as fast as Ullrich; their time splits were nearly identical.
He'd lost all the time in the last two-thirds of the race, after he'd
become dehydrated: he hadn't ridden so hard in an effort to catch
Ullrich that he'd become dehydrated; he'd become dehydrated to
the point where riding felt too hard.

That night, we sat down and I showed him the paper on which
I'd plotted out the numbers. He seemed skeptical, so I pressed.
"See," I said, "when you have fluids you are the equal of Ullrich
in the time trials—and we know you can climb better than he. So
you are the strongest."

"Not today," Lance said.

"Even today," I said. "We lost today. Yes. But because of fluid,
not because of you. Don't you see?"

He slowly began nodding his head, looking at the figures again,
absorbing what I'd told him. It was important to admit that we'd
lost—that meant we could identify a reason. Then we could build
our next victory from the ashes of our defeat.

"No matter how you feel, you are still the strongest," I said.
"There is perception and there is performance. Performance is all
that matters, all that decides the winner, yes? And if you drink, if
we defeat the dehydration, then you are once again the strongest."

He turned his head then and gave me that grin.

That night and all the next day, as he rode, I made Lance drink bottles loaded with salt, minerals, and electrolytes. We had to replenish the depleted stores his body needed. The mixtures tasted terrible.

"This is the bravest thing I've ever done," Lance joked once as I handed him another bottle.

We lost another fifteen seconds to Ullrich that stage, but the important thing was that Lance kept drinking water, absorbing electrolytes. As I watched him swig bottle after bottle as he pedaled down the road, I knew he would come back to full strength and find a way to win the Tour, to join the legendary club of five-time victors. I was certain that once he found himself back in control of his own body, he would overcome not just his dehydration but all the other problems that had seemed to nag at us since the beginning of this race. The force of that great will would be turned against the race itself, and I had witnessed that resulting in victory four times already. In a way, we were lucky that the poor time trial gave us a concrete failure to focus on—it showed us something we could fix in a way we understood and could easily accomplish. Given just that one edge over all our problems, I knew Lance would find the power then to conquer them all. But I didn't tell him that yet.

I wanted to make sure he kept drinking.

13

If You're Breathing, You Still Have a Chance to Win

I'm alive—I might as well finish the race.

A S W E R O D E over the top of the Cormet de Roselend in the 1996 Tour de France, there was the sound all around us of shifters clicking and clicking and clicking down into harder gears. Chains jumped down onto the smaller cogs we used to push our bikes to maximum speeds. There were also little bursts of ticking as some of us coasted for a few seconds while pulling on rain jackets to avoid getting hypothermic when we began rushing down the mountainside. I could see long, thin streaks of rain smashing against the pavement. But, cocooned inside the noisy boundaries of the group, I could not hear the storm itself.

I couldn't believe I was there, in the first group—among the leaders—on the second to last climb of that Tour's first mountain stage. There was the five-time Tour champion Miguel Indurain. There was the Swiss superstar Tony Rominger, Indurain's dogged rival. There was Jan Ullrich, who would go on to win the jersey for best young rider in this Tour, his first, then win the yellow jersey outright the next year before becoming, famously, Lance's fiercest competitor.

It was my first year on Rabobank, and I was supposed to be the GC (general-classification) guy—the racer who aims at the podium or, at least, the top ten overall, while capturing enough TV time and newspaper and magazine photos to justify the sponsor's cash outlay. That was a lot of pressure for a lunchbucket rider like myself. On top of that, I hadn't been feeling great since the Tour had begun. I wasn't losing much time. My fitness was okay. I'd had some good races just before the Tour. I just hadn't felt . . . right.

Until we came over that crest on stage 7.

Normally, I wasn't in the mix during the first big mountain stage of any Tour. I was one of those riders who became better as the Tour went on, who had to survive the early mountains and make gains later, picking and choosing my moments to be strong as the others weakened and lost their focus.

But there I was, in the rain and wind, with the biggest names in the sport. We had to get down this hill, then climb one more mountain to the finish. I had a chance to reach the end of the day in the top ten—and to spike up through the overall standings.

We began shushing down the slope like skiers, leaning our bikes at crazy angles in the corners, skittering across gravel the storm had washed out onto the road. Our brakes floundered—the rims of the wheels were so wet that when you squeezed the brakes, for several seconds the pads did nothing more than squeegee water off the spinning metal surface. Anyway, none of us wanted to brake much, no matter how dangerous it was—lose ground on the descent and you would have to burn valuable energy to catch back on to the group on the next mountain road.

Rominger was just in front of me, our whirling wheels not even inches apart. Spray from his tire rooster-tailed into my eyes, across my face. I blinked hard and fast and shot water out my nose, turned my head and spit and spit and spit. Pebbles and stones flew up from the road—flung out at 50 mph by our madly spinning tires. This was the sport of cycling at its most dangerous. And best.

I loved my job.

How had I become this lucky, to do this odd thing for a living?

Like the rippling movements of a snake, the line of racers swung out to the right, the movement starting from the front and each of us in turn following, setting up to carve tight across the left-hand corner coming up. We leaned our bikes over hard, pushing down with all our might against the outside pedal to drive the rubber of our tires down through the wetness and onto the pavement, praying for traction. And Rominger lost control.

His bike slid out, traction gone, the rear wheel starting to swing crazily right, to the outside of the turn. On pure instinct I'd flicked my bike right, keeping my front wheel away from his bike. Rominger slid wider, and I arced out right again, operating in that primal, instantaneous mode of reaction that rises from the sheer need to survive.

Rominger stayed up.

So did I.

We were going to make it through this wild turn.

I was going to finish with the leaders.

Gravel.

As I rode onto it, the bits of broken road and slimy pieces of stone slid sideways across the pavement, carrying me with them, and I knew I was going off the road. Time became that slow-motion, freeze-frame series of images that happens during a crisis. I had a way out. I could save myself. All I had to do was straighten up my bike, slide way back off the saddle, and clamp down on the brakes as hard I could. I'd go off the road, but slow enough to avoid getting hurt, slow enough to probably be able to get back on my bike—if I fell off at all—and maybe even try to catch the group before the finish.

Then my front wheel hit a big rock on the shoulder of the road. My bike vaulted forward, the rear wheel snapping up over my head and around, and now with time slowed I could see passing below me the twenty-inch-high stone retaining wall that lined the side of the road. Then I flew past that and off the edge of the cliff, and I hung in the air, feeling motionless, weightless, stopped in time, a hundred feet above the trees and bushes that clung to the steep, jagged incline.

I had a lot of time to think. I thought: *I rode off a cliff!*
I thought: *Well, this is going to be very bad.*
I thought: *I'm dead.*

History books will tell you that the seventh stage of the 1996 Tour de France is notable because a great champion cracked.

Miguel Indurain had won the Tour de France every year since 1991, and in his day he was as dominating as Lance; the rider known as Big Mig destroyed everyone in the time trials, and though he could not instantly crack apart the race in the mountains the way Lance was able to, Indurain would simply keep turning the pedals over and over in a big gear, grinding away most of his rivals or limiting his losses to the pure climbers. He never lost more ground than he gained in the time trials, which turned out to be a recipe for a champion.

I'd always liked Indurain. He was a quiet, big man, not given to showy theatrics, bragging, or antics on the bike. He just won.

He was a patron as powerful as Lance, or Bernard Hinault or Eddy Merckx or Jacques Anquetil, the other five-time winners of the Tour. Yet he never forgot that he came from humble beginnings—a Spanish farmer's son—and no matter how many Tours he won or how much money he made, he always told everyone that when it was over he wanted nothing more than to escape the spotlight and become a farmer himself, once again working the land in the small village of Villava, as he had as a boy. And that's just what he did.

Victory, success, fame—they never became cages for Indurain.

I also like Indurain because he was one of the very few people who believed in what Lance and I were trying to do. Before Lance was a Tour de France champion, back when we were still training, he ran into Indurain one day before a race. Indurain asked Lance what his plans were now that he'd recovered from cancer. Lance told him we were training to win the Tour de France. Indurain—like everyone—was surprised, if not shocked. But later that year, when he was asked by reporters who he thought would win the 1999 Tour, after a long, thoughtful pause—like a farmer asked to predict a crop's bounty early in the spring—Indurain said, "Lance Armstrong."

He had no reason on earth to believe in us. I was always grateful that he did.

But that was still three years in the future.

By the time we crested the Cormet de Roselend in the 1996 Tour, we had been riding through miserable, wet, windy, and cold weather for seven days. More than thirty riders had already dropped out—one of them was a young Lance Armstrong, who quit during the sixth stage, feeling sick, hacking, afraid he was catching a cold, and unaware that in a few months he would be diagnosed with the cancer that was doubtless already in his body.

Alex Zülle—the man who at times would be my team leader and in other years would be the man relentlessly chasing Lance as the two of us engineered Tour wins—crashed twice in stage 7 and finished with his clothes in tatters, his skin streaking with blood in the relentless downpour. Indurain avoided falling, but something worse happened to him: he fell apart.

The champion had never liked or ridden well in cold, rainy weather. On top of that, he'd been at the peak of the sport for five years, a long time to push your body to the extremes of training necessary to win the Tour. All of this stress began to exact its toll in stage 7. For the first time, Indurain appeared vulnerable, unable to grind his way back to the little climbers who kept jumping away from him in frenzied attacks. His pedal strokes became choppy and uneven. He seemed dazed. Desperate, at one point he begged for drinks from his support car, taking cola in an area where team cars were prohibited from feeding the riders—willing to accept a twenty-second penalty to avoid total collapse. But even with the energy boost from the soda, Indurain would finish three minutes behind the leaders, losing ground to a series of vicious attacks on the last climb, as those who had shadowed him for years sensed that the reign was over.

Afterward, Indurain himself, in his characteristic honest, understated way, would say, "My heart was willing. But my legs told me no."

I just kept hanging there.

A motorcycle TV crew happened to be alongside us at that point. I have watched the film, and I know, of course, what I have always understood logically: I simply catapulted over the wall and vanished over the side of the precipice. But in my memory, I hang there.

I looked down at the tree for what seemed like a long time. I had no more thoughts. I was not planning ahead, thinking about how to tuck and roll, whether I should grab a branch or try to land feet first.

I hung there, caught between two worlds.

The leaders sped down the mountain. On TV, a commentator cried, "It's Bruyneel riding over a cliff! Across a ravine! Johan!"

Then I was in a tree. I was kind of falling and clambering down it at the same time, climbing upside down toward the ground through green leaves and brown branches, all around me the fresh, fragrant smell of the tree. The next thing I remember is my head hitting something hard as I fell the last few feet or inches—I have no idea—out of the tree and onto the ground. I'd landed on a rock. The ground dived sharply away from me.

And there was my bike, beside me.

I seemed not at all amazed to find my bike right there at my side after a hundred-foot plunge off a cliff and a scrambling fall through a tree. It was like: of course that's what happens when you ride off a cliff. Maybe because my bike was there, my first reaction was to get back up to the road so I could get on it again. I thought: *I'm alive—I might as well finish the race.* I was moving, clattering up the side of the cliff on all fours, using my hands and feet to scrabble upward. Loose dirt and rocks rushed under me. Brush gave way. I carried my bike as if it were an injured friend I had to drag to safety.

On the TV footage, I look very skinny, and young. I am dressed in bright orange. My cycling cap is still on my head—we didn't wear helmets in those days. I look like I'm in a hurry, not scared for my life but scared that I will miss the next pack coming by. The camera is being held over the stone wall and pointing down, and the pitch of the mountainside is dizzying. The voices of my team director and mechanics can be heard—my team car had been flagged down. The owner of the team happened to be in the car that day, and when I got close enough to the top it was he who reached over and pulled me up and out of the ravine.

There was Viatcheslav Ekimov, standing astride his bike, waiting for me. He was my teammate then—this warhorse of a man who would go on to help Lance win some of his Tours before working for our team as one of the directors. Someone had already taken a spare bike off the top of the car; it was shoved into my hands and without thinking I swung my leg over the top tube and Eki and I shot off down the hill.

We descended like madmen, taking more risks than I had when I was with the front group. Neither of us talked. We rode. I was not yet scared, had not yet absorbed what had happened. We plummeted down the road.

There were about six miles of flat road between that descent and the last climb, and when we hit the flats Eki began pounding away at his bike, driving us along the road like a two-person locomotive, an engine and a caboose. We started to ride up among cars and support vehicles, which meant we'd caught the pack. We weaved through the traffic, passing cars in a blur, and came up onto the last climb. Just as the road began to tilt upward, I began to realize that I had flown off a cliff.

I had gone off a cliff.

A cliff!

It was as if my entire body realized what had happened, and I began to shut down. It was strange: On the treacherous descent, I'd taken chance after chance with Eki, tearing down the hill, never touching my brakes, giving all I had just to catch up with the group. Now that the speed was slowing, and now that the group was right there in front of us, my body rebelled. I summoned one last burst of energy and rode alongside Eki and said, "Go. Don't wait for me. I'm done."

In the long history of the Tour de France, only three men have died while racing: there is Lance's teammate, Fabio Casartelli, who crashed in 1995; the English rider Tom Simpson, who died of heart failure (later ascribed to amphetamine use) while climbing Mont Ventoux in 1967; and the Spanish racer Francesco Cepeda, who rode off the side of the Col du Galibier in 1935. (In 1910, a French racer named Adolphe Hélière drowned while swimming during a rest day.)

I could have been the fourth, but I wasn't. Why? Why not? To what end? Lance says he'd have won no Tours if I'd died that day. The death of Indurain's stony dominance would have come to seem like a minor tragedy rather than the major news it became. The next time you don't win, ask yourself what is truly a loss.

A decade after I rode off the side of Cormet de Roselend, I drove up to the spot in one of our team cars. We were using the road for training, and I was scouting out the route before the team came along. I had a passenger: Eki, who'd become one of our team directors.

We stopped the car and sat there for a moment, listening to the engine tick. The wind blew across the exposed face of the road, rustled the tree branches.

Eki said, "We rode pretty fast, yeah?"

"Yes," I said. I'd ended up losing something like eight minutes on the last climb, but I stayed in the race. There'd been a sharp, burning pain in my leg I ignored, and the next day I'd been sore and achy, as if I'd just gotten over the flu. I'd ridden for two more days, then had to quit, because I'd been unable to walk, let alone pedal. I'd torn the muscles throughout my legs.

We opened the car doors and got out and walked to the edge of the cliff. The retaining wall was tinier than I remembered. The dropoff sharper. We stood there, looking down, then out, across at the next mountain and the tiny roads we could see wrapping around the peaks.

Two memories rose up before me. The first one was funny.

In Lance's last Tour de France, in 2005, we'd come over this road. Thom Weisel, one of the owners of the team, had been in the car with me, and he'd wanted me to point out the site of the crash to him. Because of the TV footage, my crash had become iconic among followers of pro racing—in the aftermath of the crash, the attention it brought me has been much more enduring, and more influential, than the physical harm; two weeks after the crash I was healed, riding the Olympics and finishing out the rest of my season. In fact, when I landed at the airport in Atlanta, there were people rushing up to me because they'd seen me launch off the cliff on TV. Lance has said he liked the toughness I showed that day, that it stuck with him when he thought about who would be a good director for his team.

I'd pointed to the corner and said to Weisel, "Here it is," and started trying to tell him how it felt to hang there for so long. I drove around the corner as I told the story and ran full gas into another team car that had stopped for some reason. There was a terrible crunch, the screech of metal. Steam rose from the hood of our car. I turned to Weisel and said, "I don't think this is my lucky spot."

Then there was the second memory.

When I was eighteen, I was training in northern France. I liked the hills there, and I knew I needed to climb if I ever wanted to be anything more than an amateur racing star from Belgium. I was riding hour after hour, up and down the hills, putting as much elevation into my legs as I could stand.

I always tried to descend as quickly as I could, not so much for the fun—although I did love the thrill, the rushing air, the feeling of flight and freedom—but so I could get to the next hill. I was intent on improving, on reaching the next level. I wanted to be a star. A champion.

It began raining as I descended a steep hill. I stayed off the brakes, whooshing through corners, trusting my handling ability, full of the invincibility of youth. I was going so fast that I could see a big army truck up ahead growing instantaneously larger and larger in my sight as I gained ground on it. I veered out to pass the truck.

And there was a car.

Coming right at me.

I pulled back on the brake levers with all my might and, at the same time, stabbed my hips to the right, not so much turning as jerking my bike back across the road. I flew the full width of the pavement and smashed into a ditch.

When I woke up, I realized I could not open my eyes. I heard voices: "Pick him up. Pull him out. Help him."

I wanted to scream out, "No! I'm hurt. Don't move me." But I could do nothing except listen.

Boots tramped around the ditch, and clothes rustled. I could hear metal things knocking against each other. The army truck must have stopped. The soldiers were arguing about how to help me: "Pull him out of those bushes. Make sure he is breathing."

Then a car door slamming shut, footsteps running fast and hard on the ground, and a new voice, out of breath: "I am a doctor. Stop. Do not move this man. Do not touch him."

I had broken the last vertebra in my back, the D-12, and a piece of it had slid loose and touched a nerve. If those well-meaning soldiers had pulled me out of the bushes, I'd have been paralyzed for life. Or dead.

As it was, I was in a wheelchair for two months. I was not depressed—perhaps I was too young for that. I was impatient to get back to my destiny. With the arrogance of youth I took my recovery for granted. And it did come, though not without cost. Doctors had to put metal plates next to my spine to fuse some of the vertebrae, then go back in a year later and take the plates out. In the process, five of the vertebrae became inflexible, and three of the disks were damaged permanently. Throughout my pro career, and to this day, I live with the pain from that crash.

And it was that wreck, finally, that drove me off the bike at the

end of my career—that long-ago, nontelevised, noniconic private disaster that created the circumstances that led me to become
Lance Armstrong's friend and coach. It was that crash into a ditch
—not the dramatic plunge off a cliff—that defeated me after all
those years, thus leading me to a place in life where I could accomplish as team director what I could never do as a rider.

We stood there, Eki and I, and he said, "What was it like, then,
hanging out there?"

"It was nothing," I said. "It was nothing at all, not really."

14

Build the Foundation of Victory During Defeat

*We had to wear the yellow jersey for at least one day.
This was not some kind of symbolic gesture. I wanted
tangible proof that we could still wrap our hands
around what most mattered.*

SINCE 1999, the color yellow had been the lifeblood of our team. From the first time he pulled on the *maillot jaune*, on the first day of his first postcancer Tour de France, to the last time he donned one, on the last day of the last Tour of his career in 2005, Lance wore the jersey a total of eighty-three days. (He is second on the all-time list only to the great Eddy Merckx's ninety-six.) Though our team had switched primary sponsors, from U.S. Postal Service to Discovery Channel, and changed uniform designs yearly to accommodate new secondary sponsors—thus switching our hues from shades of blue to near-gray and finally to green —every one of us from mechanic to superstar rider knew that one color defined us.

More than any other team, we—and I especially more than any other director in history—planned, and judged, and, it's accurate to say, risked our whole season for the chance to wear yellow. In 2006, our first year without Lance, I couldn't kid myself about our chances of wearing our beloved color when the overall winner stood atop the podium on the Champs Élysées in Paris: no better than anyone else's. It was not a spot I liked to be in.

It's not that we were floundering in 2006. For the previous three seasons, assistant directors Dirk, Sean, and I had been working overtime after our overtime to reinvent the team for this transition. We milled through the mobs of racers at the start lines of every race, introducing ourselves to the young riders and talking with old friends — the by-now grizzled vets, some of whom were old enough to have known us when we'd raced — about who they thought showed promise. We analyzed videos of races we'd been to, and strained our eyeballs into bleariness watching streaming webcasts of those we hadn't. My BlackBerry scrolled out text messages like a teletype machine in an old movie. I'd set two recruiting goals, each one a completely different path. But I wanted us to follow them simultaneously.

The most direct solution would have been to replace Lance with another rider who could be expected to dominate the Tour. There were plenty of contenders out there — top racers who had a legitimate shot at the podium now that Lance had retired, guys like Floyd Landis, Levi Leipheimer, Alexander Vinokourov, Alejandro Valverde, Andreas Klöden. But our team already had riders at that level: Paolo Savoldelli, who'd won the Tour of Italy for us in 2005; Yaroslav Popovych, who won the best young rider jersey at the 2005 Tour de France while riding in support of Lance; José Azevedo, who'd finished fifth in the 2004 Tour de France while tearing himself apart in the mountains for Lance; and our stalwart, go-to man George Hincapie, a former sprinter who over the course of transforming himself into Lance's right-hand man on the road had ended up winning a stage in the mountains during Lance's last Tour. The problem was that, when it came to winning the Tour, all of those riders, including ours, were maybes or mights. To completely build a team around one rider and one race, you need a leader who feels as much like a sure thing as you can get in a sport where the sniffles or a car running a stop sign on a training route can erase a year's worth of work.

With Lance retired, there was only one racer in the world in that elite category—and he stood in the middle of a minefield.

In the 2005 Tour de France, the only rider who could even stay near Lance in the mountains was twenty-seven-year-old Ivan Basso, who eventually finished second overall. Six feet tall and only 150 pounds, the handsome Italian had been steadily progressing up through the overall standings: third in 2004 (with a stage win in the mountains, ahead of Lance), seventh in 2003, and eleventh in 2002 (when he won the white jersey for best young rider). His mother had died of pancreatic cancer in 2005, and he raced wearing a yellow LIVESTRONG bracelet (the fundraiser started by Lance that has raised more than $70 million for cancer survivorship). Basso liked Lance, and me, but he was tied into his contract with his current team, CSC—which felt like bad luck initially but turned out to be a fortunate circumstance for us. In the summer of 2006 Basso became embroiled in the high-profile Operación Puerto doping investigation. Spanish police had raided the office of Dr. Eufemiano Fuentes, turning up journals, notes, blood bags, and other evidence that Fuentes was providing illegal performance-enhancing drugs and blood doping to as many as two hundred professional athletes, with as many as fifty of them rumored to be cyclists. Basso and eight other riders named in the investigation were banned from that year's Tour. I was stunned, saddened for the sport, not sure the bans were entirely fair (some of the riders were later cleared of involvement), and, though it was difficult to admit to myself, I also felt an odd sense of relief, as if I'd inadvertently missed a ride in a friend's car that had ended up getting in a crash. Basso was maintaining his innocence, but whether he was clean or not, the cold fact was that he was unable to race the Tour de France in 2006—which would have been a disaster for us had we signed him and built our team around him.

Our second recruiting plan assumed—correctly—that we would not be able to sign a rider who was capable of winning the Tour de France in our first year without Lance. We needed, instead, to assemble a roster of riders who were focused not solely on the Tour, who could do well at races throughout the year and around the world. I thought this was important — to keep winning in some form while we rebuilt. Winners need to be in the habit of winning, even if the scale changes. If we simply carried on as we had when we revolved around Lance, our intense focus on that single, unreachable goal would turn us into a team that would become either used to losing, or else so discouraged that we no longer knew how to win when our time came. Both our team system and the set of expectations we'd developed specifically to win the Tour de France with Lance worked only with him, and only with a squad organized to serve him (or another overwhelming, dominant racer).

We signed the most promising youngsters we could find. In ways that are important and well respected in pro cycling but not much covered by the mainstream media, our gambles paid off. A young Russian national champion, Vladimir Gusev, would win the best climber jersey in the Tour of Switzerland at age twenty-three. The under-twenty-three world time-trial champion, Janez Brajkovic, came to us and, at age twenty-two, would win the Tour of Georgia overall (and simultaneously its best young rider jersey). We took some long-shot chances on unknown talent, too — the sort of who-knows-what-might-happen decisions, made mostly on gut instinct, that no other team in the world would even think to try. In 2005 we signed a young racer named Fumiyuki Beppu, one of the only Asian cyclists racing in Europe and the only Japanese racer working at the top level. He wouldn't have made the team without world-class talent, but I also thought he might give us a way to find an entirely new talent pool — and set of fans. I was right: Beppu was like a rock star in his homeland; when we posted his first video on our team website it attracted so many viewers, the server crashed. We'd also end up signing Li Fuyu, the first Chinese rider to ever reach the top level of the sport.

Considering that we'd just lost the greatest Tour de France racer ever, we were already having a season most teams would be happy with. (And our good results would continue right up to the end of the year: we'd finish with a stage of the Tour of Italy; the King of the Mountains jersey, two stages, and the best-team-overall title at the Tour of Spain; national championship titles in the United States and three other countries; two stages of the Tour of California—more than twenty victories in all.) Plus, we had a real shot at landing George, Paolo, Yaroslav, or José on the podium and perhaps even winning a stage or two.

But I knew we needed something more. We needed that yellow jersey.

Almost for sure, I thought we wouldn't have it when the race finished up in Paris. But I believed that we had to wear the yellow jersey for at least one day. This was not some kind of symbolic gesture. I wanted tangible proof—for myself and the team—that we could still wrap our hands around what most mattered, that we hadn't fallen so far that the most hallowed trophy of the sport was out of reach. Seeing Lance in yellow so often, we had taken for granted, just a little bit, the magic of the jersey. For most professional cyclists, a single day in yellow is the peak of their careers. Pull it over your head just one time and you are forever afterward recognized as one of those select few cyclists who have worn the yellow jersey. Possessing it can define a part of your identity always. Wearing yellow a single time is like earning a doctorate; the title never leaves you. It is a precious, rare, unending gift.

We needed the yellow jersey. And I thought George might be able to get it for us right away.

The prologue of the Tour was a flat, 4.4-mile time trial with a lot of turns through the city of Strasbourg—what racers call a "technical course." Because there would be a lot of braking and accelerations, I thought the prologue favored someone who generated a lot of power quickly rather than the time-trial specialists (who excel at bringing their bikes up to a very high speed and holding it there for extended periods). The twisting, turning course, and the tight lanes it wound through, also seemed as if it would favor riders with amazing bike-handling skills, rather than those who'd practiced lying flat out over their aero bars for hours at a time.

The sun was shining brilliantly on the Square de Tivoli the

morning of the prologue, but the morning was neither hot, nor cold—perfect racing temperature. There was a slight wind, perhaps 6 mph, no more, that would at times push the riders along the course, but after a few turns in the final mile would blow directly into their faces.

"George," I said. "Give me eight minutes—eight minutes all out—and you will be in yellow."

He nodded, his angular features jutting out and joining in intense angles.

"Yellow," I said, just the one word.

In time trials, the riders start in reverse order—the lowest-placed go off the ramp first, with a specific gap between each (usually one minute). For the prologue, because there are no standings yet, the riders start in reverse order of their best-placed finisher from the previous year. This was a big advantage for us—it meant that George could go last; everyone else's time would be in; he would know exactly what it would take to win.

About two hours into the prologue, just as the wind was picking up and blowing trash and papers across the city streets, a muscled sprinting specialist from Norway, Thor Hushovd, took over the fastest time with an eight-minute, seventeen-second ride—an average speed of nearly 32 mph. About three minutes after Hushovd finished, George left the start ramp. All of the directors, coaches, top riders, and experts had been predicting that it would take a 7:50 to win. That seemed unapproachable in this wind. Maybe 8:15 was as good as it was going to get.

We use a different radio setup for time trials. For simplicity's sake, the riders can only hear me; they can't speak back. I kept a steady stream of my trademarked calmly urgent patter flowing into George's ears: "Come on, George. Brake up here then jump and pound pound pound pound. Eight minutes, George. All out. Quick spin. Quick spin. Yellow. Yellow, George. Give me more here, more more more more. Slow for the left . . ."

George was pushing a huge gear, and his tongue, as it does during his most intense efforts, hung out of his mouth and sideways.

He was giving it everything. He wanted it as bad as I did—maybe worse. Only three Americans had ever worn yellow in the history of the Tour—Lance, Dave Zabriskie, and the three-time winner Greg LeMond. George wanted to be the fourth. At each point of the course, he was right at Hushovd's times, despite the wind. We came up onto the final straightaway, a tunnel of cheers and screams, and George drove his bike forward—threw his bike across the line at the last instant in a bid to gain every last shred of time there might be.

Can any of us really imagine what seventy-three-hundredths of a second feels like? Is it a finger snap? The literal blink of an eye? To us, it felt like a canyon. George had finished seventy-three-hundredths of a second out of yellow.

The jersey felt as if it were a million miles away. Hushovd was a pure sprinter, and the next stages were sprinter's stages—long, flat, set up with finishes on wide streets so the tangled bunch of sprinters could hurl themselves along at 40 to 45 mph. Because George had an outside shot at the podium, I didn't want to risk letting him get mixed up in that brawl. The course did have three intermediate sprint points—in the towns of Saverne, Plobsheim, and Kehl, riders who won sprints would earn points toward the green jersey; the first three riders would also earn time bonuses of six, four, and two seconds.

"There's no way Hushovd is going to give those up to you," I told George that night at dinner. "He'll either have this team going all out for it, or they'll let a break get away to eat the bonuses, just to make sure we don't swipe first."

"I know," said George.

"But just in case, right? Be ready?"

"I know," said George.

As I'd figured, Hushovd's team, Crédit Agricole, let a group escape early. Less than two miles out of the start in Strasbourg, three riders attacked and got away. They were soon joined by four more. This felt deliberate, and smart. Typically, it takes around thirty miles of constant attacks—and subsequent chases by the leader's team—before a group gets away that, for one reason or another, is acceptable to the peloton. In this case, none of the riders in the breakaway were close enough to Hushovd to steal his jersey by earning time bonuses. Neither were they the kind of dangerous, powerful diesels that might be able to make a gap stick, nor the kind of savvy breakaway specialists who might be able to figure out how to stay in front of the pack for the remaining 107 miles. Hushovd felt confident he and his team could give the break a five-minute gap or so—making sure they'd eat up the time bonuses yet still staying close enough to be caught before the finish.

The head of the peloton turned the green of Crédit Agricole, with Hushovd's yellow jersey singing brightly out from their center. They monitored the gap well, dragging the pack along fast enough to discourage further escapes, while seesawing the breakaway's advantage between four and five minutes. It was a rare calm stage on a sunny, gorgeous day early in the Tour when ordinarily little was at stake for us and I might have savored the peace, the beauty of the roads, the snaking line of colors in front of us, and the waves from the families picnicking alongside the pavement. But today I was edgy, alert.

About thirty miles into the stage, I remember looking over and seeing three or four amateur cyclists furiously spinning along a bike path that paralleled the road the peloton was swarming over. They were bobbing, huffing for breath, and hunched over their bikes. In the pack, the cyclists were chatting, smiling; some of them had one hand on another's shoulder; others drank, or ate, or rolled their heads as if working kinks from their necks. The amateurs vanished behind us, exhausted. The pack cruised along.

The breakaway absorbed the first sprint bonuses. Viatcheslav Ekimov needed a wheel change, so we swung to the side of the road, and the pace was so leisurely that I got out and pushed him myself, then strode back to the car and fell in behind the pack. There'd been a headwind when I'd gotten out to help Eki. It was one more fact about the stage that I routinely cataloged, out of long habit and training, though even as I stuck it into my memory of the day, I knew it was probably inconsequential. But it was who I'd become, this automatic reservoir of detail.

The second sprint bonuses went by. Back in the pack, cans of Coca-Cola were passed around. The Caisse d'Épargne team moved to the front alongside Crédit Agricole and the pace picked up.

"Hey George," I said.

"Saw it, Johan," he said. He was already moving up to take a look, just to see what was happening. It could be that some of the teams with sprinters stuck in the peloton were getting impatient and wanted to bring the breakaway back soon, to make sure their guys had a shot at winning the stage in a field sprint. Riders from Quick-Step moved to the front, then Milram, Davitamon-Lotto, and then Crédit Agricole crowding back in. The pace kicked up, and the gap between the breakaway and the pack quickly diminished to a minute and change within just a few miles, then the road turned and—they had a tailwind!

The gap was really going to drop now.

"Think we're going to get them before that last sprint," I said over the radio.

Forty seconds. Twenty-eight seconds. Twenty seconds with three miles to the time bonus.

Up in the breakaway, a rider named Walter Bénéteau attacked, dropping the six men he'd worked so long with—desperate to stay out front. The rest of the break sat up and the pack washed up around them like a wave over a sandcastle. Bénéteau did a sneaky thing, dodging in and out of the motorcycles in the caravan, stealing little drafts here and there. I admired him for it. And I didn't care if he stole the first sprint bonus. That was one less chance for Hushovd, and all we needed was one of the two remaining bonuses—either four or two seconds would put George ahead of Hushovd.

It was at that exact moment, as Bénéteau crossed the sprint line, that the pack turned itself inside out—a beautiful, violent movement that always amazes me. Colors leap off the front here and there, then the middle of the pack surges out of the opened neck and spreads wide across the road, while behind that forward motion there is a sort of inward collapse as riders from each side regroup into a new pack. There was Crédit Agricole, trying to steal the time bonuses. There was George. There was a tumult of riders. Spokes flashed in the sun. This little town, Kehl, was filled with people on the sidewalks, hanging out windows, standing atop cars and abutments, and they were all screaming. George dashed across the sprint line in the third, securing the final, two-second time bonus. He was in yellow.

It was what's known as "virtual yellow," meaning that if the race were stopped now he'd be the leader. But the race wasn't stopping. In five miles the real end would come, and if Hushovd sprinted to a top three spot there, he'd take the jersey back on the finish-line time bonuses. Once, George had been a true sprinter. He'd been at home in the elbowing, the head-butting, the aggressive wheel slashes and feints the sprinters made at 45 mph. He'd loved the shoulder-to-shoulder pushing. I could put him in the sprint and try to make our virtual yellow jersey real. More than likely, he'd be fine.

Up ahead, the sprinters' teams moved to the front, driving the pace so high the pack whistled now as it passed people, then stringing the entire Tour de France out into one single-file line of suffering and speed. Hushovd was in there, up in the top ten. So was Oscar Freire, a former world champion. Tom Boonen. Jimmy Casper. They were smashing against each other.

Put George into the risk-filled sprint in a bid for the yellow jersey today, or bide our time and wait for a safer shot?

"George," I said. "Stay out of it today."

The straightaway was lined with steel barriers that held the crowd back as if they were mad animals in a zoo, sticking their arms through, waving flags over the gutters, shaking giant green plastic hands and noisy clappers and high-pitched cowbells. The pack flew into them, blinded by the flags and their pure desire for the stage win, and the sprinters wound up and shot forward—Boonen, then Casper and Robbie McEwen and Erik Zabel and with them Hushovd and our yellow jersey.

Hushovd went down. There was that instant, speed-of-instinct ripple away from something that means the racers are trying to avoid a crash. In the center of it lay Hushovd. Against the yellow of the jersey, the black of the road, bright blood spurted out. In seconds he was as much red as yellow. The jersey was ours now.

But at what price?

It turned out to be almost funny. Hushovd, trying to get to the front, had ridden so close to the barriers that one of the plastic green hands had slashed across his upper arm, opening a shallow, two-inch cut. It was sort of like a giant paper cut, but the sprinter's heart rate was so high that blood literally erupted like a geyser from the minor wound. Aside from a bruise and the scare, Hushovd was unharmed.

"Yes!" I shouted when I saw George at the finish, taking him in my arms. "Yes yes yes yes yes yes yes yes yes!"

We would lose the jersey the next day — again declining to put one of our podium hopefuls amid the insanity of the final sprint. And ten stages later, when the first decisive climbs came in the Pyrenees, we would lose all of our podium hopes as well. George would bonk — fall apart as Lance had done on Joux-Plane in 2000 — and lose more than twenty-one minutes. Our best climber, Azevedo, would lose 4:10 to the leaders, Popovych, 6:25. Savoldelli would crash on a descent, open up a wound that took fifteen stitches to close, and give up more than twenty minutes as well. It would be the most disastrous day our team had ever experienced.

One day in yellow — what can that possibly mean stacked up against the previous eighty-three?

It meant everything.

In our darkest year, that speck of color kept something alive for all of us. Was it given to us by a giant plastic green hand of fate? Or was it a cunning time-bonus sprint midride? Or the fact that I registered the presence of a breeze when I got out to help Eki? I would say that sole day in yellow was the accumulation of everything that it takes to succeed in the Tour de France, all that you need to muster to be a winner in the greatest race on earth even when you know you're not going to win.

/// PUTTING IT ALL TOGETHER

15

"It Was My Dream"

*The loss is in the past, which cannot be changed.
The win — it still lies up ahead, waiting for us, and it
will stay there until we figure out how to take it.*

G ATHERING THE TEAM for our first big training camp of the
year, in mid-January, is an occasion not of hope but, more accurately, of optimism: the entire season lies before us — ours
for the taking if we are willing to work hard enough, and think
enough, and sacrifice enough. (And also, I never forget, if we are
helped along by a little luck, too: no crashes the week before a big
Classic, no sore throats or head colds in the middle of an important stage race, no mad dogs dashing into the pack in front of our
wheels, and on and on.)

In those first days of the year when we are all together, as the
riders are stretching out their legs in the parking lot before the
customary 10:00 A.M. group ride, we still might accomplish anything — or everything. The bikes are brand-new, the clothes are
so fresh some of them have yet to be laundered the first time,
still smell of the plastic package they just came out of. There is
a unique kind of spring to the riders as they jump out of their
saddles to climb a hill, or jostle with each other in make-believe
sprints. Though we have won nothing yet, our potential to become
winners is unlimited. I love the atmosphere of training camp, the
emotion, the promise.

In 2007 we met for the fifth straight year in Solvang, California. I chose this odd little city for many reasons. It is a Scandinavian-themed tourist town, which made the European racers feel a little more at home. The surrounding Santa Ynez valley supplied us with leg-cracking hills and flat, easy roads to spin along. The restaurants served good food in a variety of cuisines without being so cutting edge or trendy that an unusual dish for dinner might induce stomachaches or indigestion that might cost us the next day's training. In fact, what I appreciated most was that as a team we had settled in at Solvang. We stayed at the Royal Scandinavian Inn each year, and each year we set up our trucks and work stands in the rear parking lot, where out in the sun (and often well into the dark) the mechanics would happily toil away—fine-tuning the thirty or so new road and time-trial bikes, and applying layer after layer of heady-smelling glue to fasten our new, lightweight tires to carbon wheels. Our *soigneurs* and assistants would set up crates filled with a week's worth of energy bars, gels, water bottles, energy drinks, sodas, and snacks—you'd think a grocery store had bought the lot and was moving in. We took our team photos on the reliably scenic Alisal River Golf Course, which meant we never had to forfeit any training time in a search for photogenic locations. We had twenty-mile loops, forty-mile loops, all-day epics already scouted out and mapped—or, in the case of some of our longtime riders who'd been coming for years, memorized. After five camps, the residents had grown used to us; though each morning we could count on greeting a crowd of fans armed with cameras for arm-around-the-shoulder shots, and pens for autographing posters and caps—and a few hardcore amateur cyclists who'd respectfully tag along just off the back of our pack during rides—we never felt mobbed.

With twenty-eight riders from fifteen countries on the team in 2007, I thought it was especially important that the training camp be as routine as possible. I wanted the veteran riders to feel as comfortable as if they were slipping into their favorite pair of jeans, and I hoped that the new riders would be put at ease seeing how relaxed the others were.

But one of our new riders was so full of ease—and confidence—that I almost didn't know what to make of him.

Another one of our training camp rituals was that the team directors—Dirk, Sean, Eki, and I—would gather in one of the secluded, quiet sitting areas of the hotel and call each rider in for a private meeting. Over the winter, I'd have made up a schedule of races that I thought each rider should do; the other directors critiqued it, we made changes, swapped races around, plugged different riders into different situations, and, after literally hundreds and hundreds of hours of scheduling, we came up with a master plan for the season—for each and every rider. The schedule didn't just list races either. We could tell a rider that we expected him to win a certain race, or to try for a podium spot, or that he would be expected to ride in support of a teammate who had a better chance to win, or that he might just do the race as part of the overall training plan—to work on time trialing, for example, or on thriving in back-to-back mountain stages.

In January 2007, for instance, George Hincapie knew that he would race the Tour of California in February as a support rider, and perhaps try to win a stage; then he would go to Paris-Nice in mid-March to ride support but mostly to tune his fitness for Milan–San Remo in late March, in which we thought he might be able to win or podium; in the beginning of April, he knew, he would be riding the Three Days of De Panne in Belgium, to acclimate for the rough, gritty conditions he was sure to face in what we considered the heart of his season—the three great Classics of the Tour of Flanders, which began just three days after De Panne ended, Ghent-Wevelgem on April 11, and Paris-Roubaix just four days later. After that beating, George would recover through May until the eight-day Dauphiné Libéré in France in June, which would be an ideal practice run for him for the Tour de France in July—for which he knew he was going to be counted on as our number one lieutenant. George also knew that in the Classics he could count on the support of the Aussie hard-man Matt White, a bulldoggish Lithuanian named Tomas Vaitkus, Stijn Devolder from Belgium, and Benjamín Noval, a Spaniard who seemed as unstoppable and steady as a locomotive in the toughest one-day races.

It's a level of detail that is unmatched in the sport. But it is worth every mind-numbing, second-guessing, finger-aching, eye-straining, computer-crashing second I put into it. From 1999 to 2005, it was one of the key reasons every rider arrived at the Tour ready to help Lance win seven in a row. In 2006, it helped us salvage what I knew would be a year without a Tour de France win — we won a stage in each of the Grand Tours, wore the yellow jersey, and would take more than twenty wins in all.

In 2007, I believed that we could once again win the Tour de France — once more stand atop the podium in July, where for so long it had felt like we belonged. But July was still half a year away, and I was about to run into a twenty-four-year-old kid who had his own ideas about what should happen in Paris.

Alberto Contador, a quiet, thin Spanish racer who had joined the team just before camp started, walked into the room for his meeting, sat down, and said, "I wish for my first race to be Paris-Nice."

"That's good, Alberto," I said. "We already have it scheduled for you."

Contador nodded and, as if it were the most natural thing in the world for us to hear from a near-rookie at his first training camp with the world's best team, said, "As well, I will win it."

The first time I saw Alberto Contador, he had been unceremoniously dropped from the lead group on a mountaintop finish at a race in the town of Burgos, Spain.

It was 2002, and I was there to scout out young riders, so I was intent on the lead group; as they flashed by, sweating and thrashing at each other like a pack of dogs, I tried to analyze who looked strong and, more important, who possessed an indefinable quality I could sometimes spot — like a farmer trying to judge ripeness, or a florist trying to time a plant's bloom, I was trying to forecast which of these kids might grow into greatness. I watched the leaders go by. They were fast, strong, impressive — good riders, many of them destined for many wins, I thought. I made a few mental notes.

Then I saw a whip-thin figure flashing up the road, swooping in and out of the caravan cars that were following the leaders. He must have gotten a flat or something earlier, or had some other trouble, and was now coming back, overtaking the cars, slicing around them into an open section of road, then riding up behind the next car as easily as if he were opening the throttle of a motorcycle rather than pedaling. And it was not just the speed that caught my eye: there was a fluidity that was as beautiful to me as any piece of art.

My first impression—whip-thin—has always stuck with me, because he is in many ways exactly like the image of a whip that came to my mind; he is that stringy, that quick, and, though it happens so fast the eye has trouble appreciating it, that graceful in his movement.

It was a kid who Dirk, in one of his many scouting reports, had told me to watch out for: Alberto Contador. He was only nineteen, but I instantly felt that his five-foot-nine, 130-pound frame wouldn't change much even as he aged. He would add muscle if he rode right, but never much fat; I could see that from the structure of his limbs, the narrow shelf of his shoulders, and the long, lean nature of the muscle he already had.

There were, of course, lots of kids like him. Europe was filled with teenagers who had the build—and explosive power—of a stick of dynamite, and who also had that almost supernatural ease on a bicycle that cyclists often call *souplesse* (a French term referring to smoothness of pedaling) or *sprezzatura* (an Italian term for making something extremely difficult appear easy). It was always exciting to discover one of these kids—but often ultimately disappointing, as well. They could turn out to be as fragile on a bike as they were beautiful, simply unable to withstand the mental and physical rigor of racing day after day at the top level. There was never any way to tell at this age which riders would end up translating their immense physical gifts into greatness.

At the finish, I introduced myself to Alberto—just a few words of congratulations, nothing remarkable, and I don't think either of us remembers exactly what we said. I recall thinking, as his eyes widened, that he was impressed at meeting me — Lance and I had already won three Tours de France — and that he was trying both not to show it yet also act respectful at the same time. The motion of his gloved hand as he wiped sweat from his brow, the way he unclipped his foot from his bike — there was something almost gentle about him.

And, as I was to learn as I kept in touch with him, stopping to chat or shake his hand whenever I saw him at a race through the seasons, there was an authentically gentle quality to his life. Little details would pop up that might embarrass some riders, but which Alberto told without shame: in the city of Pinto, where he lived with his parents, he told me how he used to run out onto his family's balcony after school and whistle; flocks of doves would fly onto the rails, sometimes onto his hands, cooing to be fed.

He had all the talent he'd need to become a future Tour de France champion — perhaps even to become the heir to Lance's leadership once our star left the sport — but none of us, not even he, knew whether this quiet, respectful, shockingly lean, dove-feeding physical marvel had the toughness.

All questions about that were answered on May 12, 2004. Just eighteen miles into the cold, rainy first stage of a Spanish race called the Vuelta a Asturias, Alberto was chatting with a teammate near the front of the pack when his pupils suddenly rolled up under his eyelids. His arms and legs began to convulse — yet somehow he kept pedaling on instinct — then his head snapped from side to side and both man and bicycle crashed to the pavement.

Rushed to the hospital in an ambulance, Alberto suffered a grim diagnosis: a congenital blood clot had migrated to his brain and caused a stroke. During a risky, hours-long emergency surgery, the clot was removed and the pathways to his brain were restored. Alberto says that throughout his surgery he dreamed he was riding the Tour de France. When he awoke to discover he was in a hospital recovery room, he says, he immediately wanted to explain to his parents the feeling he'd had during his dream — the depth and breadth of his love for cycling. But, of course, his brain was weakened and so it was only much later that he could even begin to speak coherently, and even then he couldn't summon the words to equal the grand visions he'd had. He could form only the simplest phrase, a cliché that instead of feeling worn resounded for him with all he'd felt while his life was being saved; his first words, then, were to his mother: "Where there's a will there's a way."

His mother knew instantly that he was talking about returning to cycling, and began crying.

Our team had never won Paris-Nice. It's a seven-stage, 780-mile-long race that more or less vertically bisects France from its capital city all the way down to the southern coastal town of Nice. It's one of those races most Americans and very few casual cycling fans have ever heard of, but which holds immense prestige for those in the know.

The honor arises both from Paris-Nice's longevity — it's been run since 1933 — and its legendary list of winners. The great champion Jacques Anquetil, a five-time Tour de France winner, won Paris-Nice five times. Eddy Merckx, the five-time Tour de France winner, who is generally considered the greatest all-around cyclist ever, had three victories at Paris-Nice. The great Classics rider Sean Kelly, who among his 198 wins could count two each at Paris-Roubaix, Milan–San Remo, and Liège-Bastogne-Liège, ruled Paris-Nice for seven consecutive years from 1982 to 1988 — an astounding record likely to be forever unmatched. Just before beginning his then-unprecedented five-year domination of the Tour de France, Miguel Indurain towered over the Paris-Nice podium twice in a row.

I'd competed in Paris-Nice a lot when I was still racing. Even though I'd never done well there — I needed more miles in my legs to flourish and was never a great early-season performer — I liked the race. It's nicknamed the Race to the Sun because the first few stages, so far north in France, are often bedeviled by cold rain, wind, or even snow. As the pack plunges south, the weather improves, until finally the champion is crowned in the final stage right on the sunny Mediterranean waterfront in Nice. The journey from a cold, harsh start to the bright, warm finish always felt like the essence of victory itself to me.

As I'd made up the 2007 race schedules before training camp, I'd calculated that Contador had a good chance to win Paris-Nice. It was only a week long, which suited young riders like him, who were more likely to wilt during the last couple weeks of the longer stage races. There were two significant mountain stages out of the seven days of racing (plus one short, three-mile time-trial prologue, as well), which created a high ratio of climbing that also suited him. And, perhaps most important, as I'd created the year's program for Levi Leipheimer, I'd concluded that it made sense for him to ride Paris-Nice in a support role.

I expected Levi to contend for the Tour de France win in 2007. Publicly, I was admitting only that I thought he had a good chance to make the podium in July. And, even to Levi himself, I stressed that we should expect to stand on the Tour's podium, but I didn't specify where; I didn't want to put too much pressure on him. But my gut feeling was that he had as good a chance as any of the top contenders to win the whole thing—if we managed his season right. In the four years between his departure from our team in 2002 and when I recruited him back at the end of 2006, I'd closely studied his performance under other directors. I thought he'd been making the mistake of getting too fit too early in the season—working very hard to be fast in late spring and early summer, which then left him unable to achieve peak conditioning for the Tour in July. My plan was to have Levi peak almost immediately for a win at the Tour of California in February (which he would end up doing), then begin to taper off. Through March, April, and May he would concentrate on accumulating base fitness—a solid foundation of relatively steady-state, low-impact miles that would prove unbreakable as later in the season we added more and more intensity on top of it through June. Finally, we'd arrive at a training peak during the Tour de France itself. He was going to be slower than he'd ever been in May, but faster than he'd ever been in July.

This was essentially the same idea that had worked seven years in a row with Lance, modified to include more racing for Levi, as well as the rest of the team. The difference with Lance was that I always knew that something would have to go horribly wrong for him not to stand atop the podium in July; in contrast, for us to get up there now, everything would have to go right. Because of that gap in certainty, I could no longer gamble our entire season on one race. (The strategy paid off, too: the team would go on to win more than forty races in 2007, our best season ever.)

But Alberto was not concerned with my big-picture ideals. He wanted to win Paris-Nice. If my planning meant that in mid-March, Levi would be ideally situated to ride in support of the young Spaniard, that was all he needed to hear. He would have a genuine, world-class star working for him. He smiled, and his brown eyes flickered. There is a serenity in his eyes that is very different from Lance's nakedly burning intensity, but you also have the unmistakable impression that something is raging behind those walls of nondescript brown.

"Okay," I said to Alberto that January day in the directors' conference, hiding my surprise at his ambition and forwardness—and confidence. "Sure. Why not all for Paris-Nice? If you're going to ride it, we might as well win, right?"

We lost Paris-Nice in stage 2.

Going into the undulating, 110-mile stage that was expected to be nothing more than a showcase for the sprinters, Alberto, Levi, and the rest of the top ten in the general classification had been separated by less than five seconds. This tight competition was what we'd expected. In a short race like Paris-Nice, the final victory is almost always decided by a few seconds rather than a few minutes as in the Tour de France.

In the last six miles, the sprinters' teams went to the front and sent the pace sky-high to chase down the remnants of a daylong breakaway. The pack slammed through the city of Limoges, career-ing through tight corners and stuffing itself into narrow streets, a hundred near-misses happening every second, and throughout the peloton sliced high-pitched beeps—the sound of limit alarms being set off as the cyclists' heart rates exceeded the ranges pro-grammed into their handlebar-mounted computers. It was high-risk, high-speed utter chaos full of failing bodies, missed signals, botched communications, and split-second reactions that could lead equally to victory or loss—pretty much business as usual for a sprint finish. And just as it all broke loose, one of our lieutenants, Yaroslav Popovych—Popo—flatted.

Two of our riders made an instant decision to drop back and wait for Popo—which was the wrong decision. In a second, our team was no longer together. Alberto and Levi found themselves in the middle of the peloton and, just ahead of them, someone wobbled, or hesitated, or braked too hard going into a turn, and the pack cracked in half.

Thirty-eight riders—the lucky, persistent, strong head of the pack—finished within two seconds of the winner. Alberto, Levi, Tommy Danielson, and around seventy other riders finished in a second group that was as much as nineteen seconds back. In Paris-Nice, that time gap might as well have been an eternity.

"I can't believe it!" Dirk shouted into my phone. He and Eki were our team directors for the race. I was shuttling between Paris-Nice and another race going on in Italy at the same time, Tirreno-Adriatico, which Yatesy was directing for us, so I hadn't been there for the stage. Dirk was livid. "Seventeen seconds!" he shouted. "Seventeen seconds behind the pack!"

"Dirk," I said.

"If you lose time because you get dropped or you're not good enough that's one thing," he said, a little quieter but in a tone that would still easily be described by anyone as loud. "But for a bad decision—for something that can be avoided—for confusion—for—for—"

I waited to hear for what.

He thundered, "You cannot have that!"

"Dirk," I said. "I'm pissed off, too. It's a stupid way to lose time. It's really disappointing."

There was silence.

"So," I said, "The loss is in the past, which cannot be changed. The win—it still lies up ahead, waiting for us, and it will stay there until we figure out how to take it. It's not going anywhere. We have to find our way to it. So how do we get that time back?"

Dirk laughed—more of a grunt, really. "Listen to this: Alberto came to me after the stage, and he said, 'It's a shame.'"

"Yes," I said. "It is."

"Then he said, 'I can still win it.'"

"Yes?"

"Yes. Johan, when are you coming?"

"Stage 4," I said. "I'll be in the car for stage 4."

"Good," he said.

"Hey, Dirk."

"Yes?"

"You know, that split would have happened even for me, even if I'd been directing. You know in that chaos it's up to the riders to come through. All we can do is prepare them for that moment and talk to them right up to that moment."

There was a silence again, much longer than the first, but somehow it felt more amiable, less heavy. Then, over my phone, Dirk's voice: "Thanks."

I'd meant what I said. After all these years, Dirk had become an exceptional team director, and it gave me great satisfaction to think that all of the things Lance and I had learned together about winning and losing would not just vanish once both of us had retired—a subject I'd been thinking more and more about since 2006. It was my job to win the Tour de France. But it was my dream to win one more without Lance—to prove to myself that I could. Once I did that, I found myself wondering, would it still feel the same—winning? Would I still feel like there was anything left to win, or would the situation be like another version of what Lance and I had felt after his record-breaking sixth win: Now what? And why? And, in truth, I wasn't so sure that after I secured victory in one Tour without Lance I'd want to keep trying to win more even if I could. I knew, by now, what it took to win: the year-round, day-long, every-minute focus on cycling. I wasn't sure I was willing to make that sacrifice anymore. I missed my family.

I was haunted by something I'd been told by a friend of mine who was as deeply involved in Formula 1 car racing as I was in cycling. He told me a story about coming home from another season and seeing a picture his young daughter had drawn of their family. There was his daughter, her little brother, their mom, and even the nanny all happy together. And far over on the other side of the piece of paper, alone, stood a cartoon version of my friend, talking on a cell phone.

I didn't want to end up on the other side of the paper in my family's life. My wife, Eva Maria, supported and encouraged me from the start to the end of every season—and that's part of what made leaving her at home so hard. I knew she believed in me, and wanted me to fulfill my dreams, even though it meant we spent more days apart than together. Once I achieved that next victory, I thought, I would reward her dedication. I wanted to make up for everything that we'd missed.

And my daughter, Victoria, who was three, deserved a father, too. I wanted to get my win and get back to my girls. More and more, when I was away from them, I found my focus interrupted at odd times by a memory of one perfect day we'd had together.

It hadn't been much of a special day at all, which made it all the more unusual for us. We didn't do anything but hang around our house: No guests, no hours-long phone call for me, no planning the next trip . . . It had come after a race season, and we'd all slept late. We had paella for lunch and, because it was hot out, we just hung around in the house, talking, telling jokes, looking at drawings Victoria had made. Around three, we started watching cartoons on TV, and all of us fell asleep.

Victoria woke me up, pulling on my arm. She was in her little kid's bikini, smiling, impatient. I put on my swimsuit and the three of us jumped in the pool out in our garden, and then we spent the rest of the day floating on air mattresses.

And that was it. We did nothing, and we did it together. And I wanted, more than anything, to do more of that.

I used to worry, now that Lance had retired, that when I quit, everything we'd worked so hard to build might just vanish — we'd be nothing but marks in a record book. It wasn't like he and I created grand buildings or majestic bridges. What would be left, I used to wonder? Now, though, I knew: Dirk was part of the answer. And Yatesy and Eki, and maybe whatever Levi might be able to pass on someday to some other fresh, smart, inquisitive racer, the same way Lance had passed his ideals to Levi.

But first we had to un-lose Paris-Nice.

When Contador attacked on the very last climb of stage 4, we could not see him from the car but one of the many radio commentators shouted, "He's having fun!"

Dirk and I looked quickly at each other and smiled, then he jerked the steering wheel hard to just narrowly miss clipping a motorcycle. I think after all these years he also drives as wildly as me.

The stage had steadily traversed uphill for the last fifty miles or so, but Dirk and I had correctly anticipated that all of the time that would be gained or lost would come in the final two miles — a withering 10-percent-grade climb to the airport in the town of Mende. In that small stretch of road, Contador's time gains on his way to winning the stage were eye-popping: thirteen seconds over world-class climber Cadel Evans; twenty-eight seconds over Frank Schleck, who won atop the legendary Alpe d'Huez in the 2006 Tour de France; nearly a minute over the wiry French racer Sandy Casar — who'd been twenty-five seconds ahead of Alberto at the base of the climb.

But a wily thirty-five-year-old Italian named Davide Rebellin took the overall lead by riding smart. "Contador was very strong," he told the press afterward. "I wasn't able to go with him, so I kept him fifty meters away." Rebellin was a formidable opponent because he could both ride and think. He'd been at the front of that split in stage 2, on the good side of that big gap. When Alberto attacked at the end of stage 4, Rebellin instantly realized that he didn't have to risk burning himself up trying to stay with the explosive climber—all he had to do was preserve as much time as he could; he'd ridden conservatively and finished just two seconds behind Alberto. At the end of the day, he held a six-second lead over Alberto. In third place, twenty-three seconds back, was a rider named Tadej Valjavec. It was a two-man race now.

But I wasn't sure we could make up those six seconds. Rebellin would not be easy to crack. In one week back in 2004, he'd won the Amstel Gold Race, Flèche Wallonne, and Liège-Bastogne-Liège—an astounding three Classics in seven days. (And a month after this Paris-Nice, he would go on to win the 2007 Flèche Wallonne.)

We went after Rebellin the next day and ended up blowing the race apart. With little fanfare, and almost incognito, Popo insinuated himself into the middle of a thirteen-man breakaway that escaped within the first five miles. Stage 5 was 110 miles with five ranked climbs, none of them higher than category 2 or steeper than 6 percent; on paper, it didn't look like an especially tough day, which might be why Rebellin's team, Gerolsteiner, let Popo join that break without chasing it down. But I thought the stage was one of those that could be made just as hard as you wanted to make it—there was just enough climbing that the stage would become exceedingly difficult if Popo dropped the hammer and forced everyone to ride near their limits.

So, as the break reached the base of the very first climb of the day, from the passenger seat in Dirk's car, I said into the radio, "Popo: full gas, full day." As hard as he could go, as long as he could go.

Popo accelerated up the hill, instantly shedding six riders and quickly increasing the breakaway's lead over the peloton to four minutes. He drove on and on across the choppy roads, head down amid the gorgeous silhouettes of almond trees. With twenty miles to go he rode away even from the break itself on the second-to-last climb.

All day, thanks to the three- and four-minute leads he'd built, he'd been the virtual leader of the race, but now with so little road left he had a real shot at taking the jersey from Rebellin; Gerolsteiner launched a blistering chase, the speed so high it lined the entire peloton out in single file. As their riders wilted, other teams came forward to help—Lotto, Lampre, Caisse d'Épargne. The speed was melting the peloton—and Popo's lead. He held on to win by fourteen seconds—our second victory in two days. The effort it had taken to chase him had whittled the main pack down to fifty riders. Stragglers were scattered all across the roads for miles behind. Gerolsteiner had been put into a state of distress; at the end of the stage, one of their riders, a kid named Heinrich Haussler who was wearing the race's polka dot jersey for best climber, told the press in exhaustion: "This was the worst day of my life."

But Rebellin had hung on, shadowing Alberto in the pack. He still had his six seconds.

"So," I said to Dirk before I left for Tirreno-Adriatico. "Again."

And again the team attacked, on stage 6, which was 124 miles with nine categorized climbs (though only one of them a category 1). Levi went with a break then, by pushing the pace in a stretch of about thirty miles that included six of the day's climbs, he absolutely decimated the race. The day was so hard that no less than eleven riders would abandon the race on the road—including four of Rebellin's Gerolsteiner teammates (one of them being Haussler).

Yet once again, the dogged Rebellin hung on. Watching the finish on live TV that day in Italy, I had to admire his determination and bravery.

There was one stage left. One chance. I played the whole race over and over in my head. I thought about the last, eighty-mile stage—a traditional loop that had barely changed since I'd ridden it back in the 1990s. It had four good climbs, three of them category 1, including the cruelly steep final ascent, the Col d'Eze.

I called Dirk. "Listen," I said. "We have to ride tomorrow as if we were already winning."

"At the front," Dirk said, already following me. "Full team."

"Exactly. Instead of attacking attacking attacking, we ride as if Alberto is wearing the leader's jersey and we are defending it. The pace is so high so long no one escapes, right? We get to Col d'Eze as a bunch and let it be Alberto versus Rebellin."

"I'll take that matchup," said Dirk.

"Yes. I'll bet Alberto will, too. And if Alberto drops him there, finally no one will help Rebellin—he has no team anymore, and it's the last climb of the race. Instead of trying to chase down Alberto to preserve their positions, the other riders will attack Rebellin to try to take over his."

"It's good," said Dirk.

Next I called Alberto. I explained the strategy, then said, "You're tired, no?"

"Little," Alberto admitted.

"Rebellin is a lot tired."

I let that sink in. I said, "I know that last climb tomorrow well. It is cruel and it is steep and it is tiring—much more so than Mende." That was the mountain on which Alberto had ridden away from the pack to his stage 4 victory. "You flew away from Rebellin in Mende. Tomorrow, there's no way he can stay with you. You will fly to victory."

Alberto laughed. "Fly," he repeated. "We will be flying."

And that is how Alberto Contador looked when he won Paris-Nice, as if he were flying up the Col d'Eze into the bright sky of the Race to the Sun, leaving the pack behind perhaps like one of his doves soaring high off while the human who dreams of flight stands grounded on the balcony.

I watched it on the small satellite TV screen mounted to the wall of our team bus in Tirreno-Adriatico: a tiny figure in blue swooping along a road. Sean was there with me, watching, and Janez Brajkovic, who'd just finished his time trial and hadn't yet showered, and the bus driver.

Dirk had done everything right. "A murderous pace!" the TV had shouted when our team was a solid wall of blue at the front, dragging the pack behind. And when Alberto had attacked: "Rebellin can't follow . . . the other riders attack *him* now!"

Alberto raised his hands to the sky as he crossed the line. Standing in a bus in another country, dancing, raising my arms myself, I screamed, and turned and hugged Sean and Janez and the bus driver. It felt not like the finish of something, but a start.

16

Everything but Winning Is a Distraction

I was still willing to risk losing to win. Something inside me would never settle for being in the middle.

How much of my life had I spent like this, in a team car? How many hours had I sat up here in the front watching a TV screen, talking to my riders over our race radios while scrolling through my text messages all at once — sometimes while also driving with my knees controlling the steering wheel? How many times had I looked in the rearview mirror and glimpsed — through a thicket of three spare wheels, two toolboxes, three cases of bike parts, twenty-nine food bags, up to one hundred water bottles, and a mound of rain jackets, gloves, vests, caps, and arm and leg warmers — the barely visible face of one of our mechanics?

Figure it out for the Tour de France alone: This was 2007, my ninth Tour de France. It usually takes around 80 to 90 hours of total saddle time for the racers to circle the country. Say it all adds up to 720 hours. That's thirty days, isn't it? One month, for a race that lasts a month. Fitting? Funny?

How about this way: one month of my life.

That's a good month — used up just right. I know I'll think that even when it's time for me to leave this life. No regrets about that month.

So goes the mind of a team director trying to distract himself at the start of what feels like the most important stage of his life: the 135-mile stage 16 of the 2007 Tour de France, at the end of which, on top of a monster of a climb called the Col d'Aubisque, I would know whether we had won or lost this Tour—whether I was a team director who had won seven Tours thanks to one rider, or whether I was a winner in my own right.

My eyes fixated on one of the saved text messages I'd been idly scrolling through: "I hope my rivals will be Valverde and Evans."

It was a reply to one of the many messages I'd sent out to our team a week before we'd met in France for the start. I'd gone over the course and the rosters again and again, then sent inspirational notes out to each rider, tailored to remind each of them what their roles and goals were for us. I thought Alberto was a near guarantee to win the white jersey, awarded to the best young rider, so I'd sent him a message outlining his rivals for the honor.

He'd quickly sent back his reply, and the meaning of it was clear. Alejandro Valverde and Cadel Evans were two of the top contenders not for the white jersey but for the yellow jersey—the overall win. Alberto had been letting me know he believed he could win the whole thing.

And now he had a chance to prove it.

Stage 16 was the last mountain stage of 2007—and our final chance to tear the yellow jersey away from Michael Rasmussen, who'd had a stranglehold on it for ten days, since the second stage in the Alps.

Rasmussen was nicknamed Chicken—either because, depending on who you chose to listen to, he loved eating poultry or he was lean to the point of scrawniness. He was a thirty-three-year-old Dane, five foot nine and 130 pounds, who'd started out as a mountain biker before turning to the road and making a name as one of the best climbers in the world. He'd won the King of the Mountains jersey twice in the Tour, in 2005 and 2006 (along with four stages) and a stage in the Vuelta a España. He was now riding for my old team, Rabobank.

As the pack set out from the town of Orthez, I could see Rasmussen near the front, resplendent and lean, surrounded by the orange-and-blue jerseys of his team. Off to the side I saw Alberto in the sparkling white jersey of the best young rider, and riding beside him Levi Leipheimer, who'd come into the race as our team leader but now found himself in the role of Alberto's lieutenant. Alberto was in second, two minutes and twenty-three seconds behind Chicken; Levi was fourth, at 5:25. (Between them was Cadel Evans at four minutes flat.)

There were four climbs standing between us and the yellow jersey. The first, and the steepest, would come less than fifty miles into the day: the *hors categorie* (HC) Port de Larrau, which *averaged* just over 8 percent for its nine miles; portions of it were nearly too steep to walk. Second up was the category 1 Col de la Pierre-Saint-Martin, which also climbed about nine miles but wasn't as steep. After thirty miles or so, the peloton—or what was left of it—would run smack into the category 1 Col de Marie-Blanque, which averaged nearly 7.5 percent for almost five miles, then, a mere ten miles later, into the cruel wall of the Col d'Aubisque, an HC beast whose ten-plus miles at 7 percent would rip the legs off most of the survivors. It was there that I knew we had to attack as if there would be no more attacks for us to give—ever.

I'd told the team as much the night before. I'm not a big pep-talk coach. I don't go in for the rousing, shouting, loud team rally. In small groups, twos and threes, I spoke to them not about strategy but about what was in my heart.

"We have done a great job of putting ourselves in a position to win," I said. "The Tour has been crazy this year. We have survived its madness and we have a chance very few people thought to give us: we can ride into Paris in yellow. But to do that we need full gas. We need all-out attacking. If we do not crack Rasmussen tomorrow, we will know that we have lost the Tour de France."

And to Levi and Alberto, who would have to do the cracking, I said, "We must ride in such a way that if we do not win, we lose. To have a chance at the top step, we have to be willing to never take one step onto the podium."

I was telling them that to take the yellow jersey they had to be willing to ride so hard it would endanger their podium spots — Alberto was solidly in second and Levi still had a shot at third. All or nothing.

No Plan B. Nothing in reserve. No save-the-day strategy. Just everything we were against everything Rasmussen was, everything the Tour de France was.

Stage 16 was going to be insane, chaotic, unpredictable, cruel, unforgiving, and punishing — and lead to unimaginable triumph or abject failure. The whole Tour de France had been that way. And not only because of the riding.

On stage 8, a racer on the T-Mobile squad, Patrik Sinkewitz, had to abandon the Tour after he broke his nose and injured his shoulder in a collision with a spectator. One of Sinkewitz's teammates, Linus Gerdemann, gave up his one-stage stint in yellow that same day. Gerdemann, a twenty-four-year-old climber who had ridden to a stage win and the *maillot jaune* in the first mountain stage, was a popular rider and a vocal opponent of doping. His victory was seen by many as proof that clean riders could not only compete but win.

"It is great to see Linus win," said an enthusiastic David Millar to reporters, even though he was not a teammate of Gerdemann's. Millar, a young Scot who was riding for Saunier Duval, had become an unofficial spokesperson for the sport. He himself had admitted to EPO use in June 2004 after police searching his home found syringes; after serving a two-year ban, he had returned to the sport vowing to help clean it up. "This is the sign of a new generation coming through," Millar said.

Two days later, it was announced that Sinkewitz had failed an out-of-competition drug test for testosterone doping in early June; he would have been kicked out of the Tour had he not already withdrawn.

Nine days after that — on the rest day before stage 16 — it was announced that testing on Alexander Vinokourov had returned an A sample that was positive for blood doping, and that he and his entire Astana team were withdrawing from the Tour. Vino, as he's called, had been one of the prerace favorites for yellow until a crash on stage 5 forced him to ride with stitches in his knees, an injury that would slow him so much his chance at yellow was over. Though he could not make up all the lost time, Vino had sought to redeem his reputation with stage wins, taking in two out of three days the stage 13 time trial and the stage 15 climb through the Pyrenees.

Rasmussen, meanwhile, was at the center of a fast-growing storm of criticism. For about a week, reports had been circulating in the media that he'd been unavailable for several out-of-competition drug tests before the Tour. (By contract, racers must make their whereabouts known at all times for out-of-competition testing; missing too many tests is considered the same as returning a positive test for doping.) At the poststage press conferences, it seemed as if Rasmussen spent as much time defending himself against cheating as he did talking about how he planned to defend the yellow jersey.

Being inside the Tour de France felt like living in a tornado zone—and getting hit by twisters every day. No one knew where the destruction was going to come from next.

Amid this disorienting, discouraging, damaging whirlwind, I did a very selfish thing: I turned the focus of our team ever harder, ever tighter, ever closer to the race itself.

"We are here to win the Tour de France," I told them at night, stopping by their hotel rooms, or as one or two of us sat at the dinner table or sipped espresso in the team bus before a start. "There is nothing we can do to prosecute the guilty or protect the innocent. That is not for us. We are here to race. We are not here to judge anyone or to try to anticipate who might be doping or not. We are here to race the Tour de France, and we are racing it because we want to win it.

"We are here to win," I would say to the team. "Until the race is over, everything but the idea of winning is a distraction."

I was used to seeing the sport's doping problems this way—as one more barrier to winning. I had more or less been trained to do this since 1999, when, after Lance's first great ride up Sestriere, the leading French sports newspaper ran a headline over the story of his exploit—"On Another Planet"—that was a sort of European code for "he must be doping, because no mere human could do what he did."

But, in truth, this time I was shielding the team not only from the outside world but from my own turmoil.

For one thing, whether you thought doping got so much attention because it had become a pandemic, or a witch-hunt, or (like most of us) something in between, there was no arguing that the entire situation—from the actual cheating itself to the policing and penalizing and publicizing of it—felt wildly out of control. T-Mobile, for instance, had been lauded for its aggressive and public antidoping stance, which included a requirement that each of its riders submit to the team's own series of frequent tests in addition to those administered by the testing agencies. It suddenly felt as if any team might one day have its own Patrik Sinkewitz, who later admitted that, almost without forethought and with no real consideration of the consequences, on his own he'd applied testosterone cream to his underarm to help himself recover during a training camp. Not a single rider on U.S. Postal or Discovery had ever tested positive for doping while on the team. Not one. I could not help but think of what might happen to the legacy Lance and I had built—and to the hundreds of thousands of cancer survivors he helped and inspired—if someday even one of our lowest-ranked riders made a mistake that ended in a positive drug test at any race in any part of the world at any time of the year.

For another thing, I myself had taken our team too close to the center of the doping controversy in the off-season.

On October 18, 2006, Ivan Basso and his team, CSC, announced that they had terminated his contract "by mutual consent," due to his ongoing involvement in the Operación Puerto investigation that had resulted in his banishment from the 2006 Tour de France. There seemed to be a lot of evidence against him, but I am a fan of the American system of justice: innocent until proven guilty. I didn't outright dismiss hearsay and circumstantial evidence, but I didn't trust it, either: three entire books full of nothing but circumstantial evidence and unsubstantiated testimony had been written accusing Lance of doping.

Our team's policy was clear and ironclad: any rider who tested positive or confessed to using performance-enhancing drugs would be off the team; it seemed fair to me to base our decisions on evidence instead of innuendo. Great example: One of the names on the first, speculative list of who'd been involved in Operación Puerto was Alberto Contador. But shortly after he was banned from the 2006 Tour (along with four other members of the team that was originally known as Liberty-Seguros, then, after reorganizing, became Astana), both the Spanish judicial system and cycling's worldwide governing body, the UCI, cleared him, saying that although his name had appeared incidentally in some of the files alongside those of his teammates, there was no evidence he had participated. Alberto, in plain language, had absolutely nothing to do with the scandal. The doctor at the center of the scandal, Eufemio Fuentes, also said he had never worked with Alberto. If I'd acted on rumor instead of reality, I'd never have signed Alberto.

Basso was claiming he was innocent as well, and nine days after he left CSC, the Italian Olympic Committee announced that, based on insufficient evidence, it was acquitting him of any charges related to Operación Puerto. (When an athlete is accused of doping, no matter which lab or agency detected the alleged infraction, the trial is conducted by his own country's Olympic committee.) We asked four different lawyers to examine the rulings, the evidence, and the UCI code of conduct riders agreed to abide by, and the legal opinion was unanimous: the documents meant Basso was free, and eligible to ride.

He was the one guy Lance and I both knew could step right into our team's leadership role to begin another dynasty. We signed him to Discovery in early November 2006; he and Levi would be our coleaders for the Tour de France. From here to the end of Basso's association with us, I must respect his privacy and stick to the public details only. In late April 2007, the Italian Olympic Committee reopened its investigation; on April 30 he and I agreed that he would leave the team, and on May 2 he appeared before the Italian Olympic Committee and admitted to "attempted doping." In June he was banned from the sport for two years. Knowing everything I do now, I have to say that I made a mistake signing Basso.

I just wished we could all get together and race bikes as if we were kids again.

On climbs, though Alberto's accelerations never look ugly, their effect on other riders is violent and destructive. He jumps like a bullet coming out of a gun — and he can fire three, four, five, six times in a few kilometers, going all out, then recovering quickly before attacking again. He's what other cyclists call, admiringly, a "pure climber." It doesn't mean that's all he can do; it means that when he climbs, he is flawless.

But despite his gifts, Alberto was still only twenty-four years old. There was a good chance the Tour would wear him down after two weeks, strip away his power until the most we could ask from him would be to finish. So my plan had been to send him out fast and hard toward the end of the first set of mountain stages, which would come in stages 7, 8, and 9. I hoped to be able to let him ride moderately when we first hit the mountains, giving him a day or two to sort his legs out, then use him to tear the race apart and soften up the contenders before he got fatigued.

And that would align perfectly with my strategy for Levi. When he'd come back to the team at the end of 2006, I'd told him I thought he could make the podium of the Tour de France — that he should have been on it already.

"I know," he said. "But something always goes wrong. I feel like one off day costs me, every time."

I'd been thinking the same thing, and as I outlined my strategy I could see his face change from registering doubt to confidence. I wanted him to start the season in worse shape, I explained. For

one thing, remember, I thought all along that he had been peak-
ing too soon over the past few seasons—getting too fast too early,
then slowing down during the Tour. "You have to accept that you're
going to be slower than you've ever been in your life in May," I
warned him. "You can't let that scare or discourage you."

And when it came to the Tour, I continued: "You have to hide.
You have to be the quietest contender. Invisible, okay? The Tour
for you is not about gaining time but about not losing time."

"Then," said Levi, "how do you ever win if you never gain
time?"

I liked the way he asked the question: he wasn't trying to pick
my idea apart but genuinely wanted an answer. "Each day in the
mountains," I said, "someone different will win and someone who
won before will fall back. Someone who finishes in front of you
one day will be behind you the next because you will never fail.
And in this way"—I paused, sliding my hand between our faces,
dipping it into a valley at our chins, and then raising it back up to
eye level—"in this way you will sneak to the top."

Gerdemann had won the first mountain stage with a long breakaway that didn't feel dangerous to our overall hopes; the contenders for the overall win—Rasmussen, Evans, Valverde, Levi, and Alberto—finished together in a trailing group, happy to mark each
other rather than Gerdemann. It felt like a warm-up. And it turned
out to be: the next day Rasmussen danced through the Alps, holding a lead over three category 1 climbs (including the Cormet de
Roselend, where I rode off the cliff) and taking the yellow jersey.

"How do you feel?" I asked Alberto that night.

"Good. Strong."

"Eager?"

"Yes." He smiled. "Of course."

"Why don't we attack tomorrow? Not to win, just to attack. To
play."

Stage 9 was tricky and hard: only ninety-eight miles, with a category 1 climb and two HCs—the first almost at the start and the
last just before a twenty-two-mile descent to the finish line (which

sat atop a short, steep uphill as well). Less than two miles into the stage, a rider from AG2R attacked, and we pounced.

"Popo, that's you," I said into the radio, and Yaroslav Popovych bridged up. "Let's make it hard today." He did, eventually being joined by a small, intense group of climbing specialists including Mauricio Soler—a twenty-four-year-old Colombian who would go on to win the stage and, in Paris, this year's polka dot jersey. Popo's breakaway had a three-minute lead on the yellow-jersey group by the time the race got to the last climb, the 10.8-mile, 7-percent-average-grade Col du Galibier.

"Okay," I said to Popo. "Now wait for Contador."

Then to Alberto: "*Vamos!*"

Alberto burst from the yellow-jersey pack. Only Evans could match the acceleration, and then only briefly before falling back. He dangled between Alberto and the yellow-jersey pack. Alberto opened space between himself and Evans, and Rasmussen, Valverde, and the others.

"Levi, *tranquillo,* right?" I said. Easy, I meant. He was sitting in the pack amid the leaders, hiding, holding back, as I'd asked him to.

Just as Popo crested, Alberto rode up onto his wheel and together they began screaming down the mountain, taking turns working together in front while the other rested in the draft. Soler was going to win, but I didn't care: behind Popo and Alberto, the leaders were shredding themselves in a desperate effort to catch our two riders. Teammates together off the front of a pack are dangerous precisely because they are teammates—unlike a breakaway made up of members of different teams, they will cooperate right to the finish line to gain maximum time. Rasmussen and his group caught Popo and Alberto before the finish, but it had been a great stage for us.

Levi had done no hard work so far, but he was sitting in ninth place, just 3:53 behind Rasmussen. Alberto was in fifth—and the white jersey—at 3:08 back.

The Tour traveled across France on flat roads and rollers for three days, then ripped through the town of Albi in the stage 13 time trial won by Vino. We entered the Pyrenees in stage 14 with Alberto in third at 2:31 back and Levi in fifth at 3:37. The stage packed two HC mountains — a total of twenty miles of climbing — into the last forty miles. Alberto and Rasmussen traded attacks on the final climb up Plateau de Beille, blowing apart Evans, Soler, Valverde, Carlos Sastre, and the rest of the pack. With half a mile to go, Alberto sat calmly behind Rasmussen, then unleashed one of his unmatchable sprints to take the stage. Levi rode in forty seconds later.

That night Levi came over to me and said, "You know Rasmussen and I were roommates sometimes when I was with Rabobank?"

"Yeah," I said.

"So we're friendly. So today after the stage he said to me, 'You should tell Contador not to ride like a little girl.' I guess he didn't like the way Alberto sat on his wheel at the end."

"Don't tell Alberto," I quickly said. It wasn't that I was afraid of hurting his feelings. I wanted to save Rasmussen's comment and use it when it might make a difference. At the same time, I found myself thinking about Levi's actions. The entire cycling world, from racers to fans, knew that Levi had been designated as our podium hope, and here he was having the best Tour de France of his life — sitting less than four minutes from the lead as he gained strength every day — yet he was finding himself overshadowed by Alberto, who was exceeding my expectations by staying strong and had a clear and better chance of winning. I could think of many cyclists on other teams who, in similar positions to Levi's, handled it by becoming bitter and divisive, creating tension within the team that sometimes grew into such a rift that no one won. Levi was not only not like that but, on his own, he'd come to me and volunteered information that might help us motivate Alberto.

He is one of the finest, noblest teammates I have ever known. He prizes winning above all, even above his own ambition.

Stage 15 was capped by an HC climb that averaged 8.5 percent for the final six miles—the steepest stretch of road in this year's Tour—and the category 1 Col de Peyresourde, which was nearly six miles at 7.8 percent. Vino escaped early in a breakaway of twenty-five riders, and would stay away to win the stage. But it was the yellow-jersey group that mattered, the top contenders riding together all the way to the base of the final climb, the mighty Peyresourde, eyeing each other like Saturday night brawlers in a pub waiting eagerly for someone to throw the first punch.

"Gas, Alberto," I said.

It was beautiful in a certain shocking way, something perhaps like the sure motion of a feeding shark. Alberto glided up out of the group, and only Rasmussen, crawling all over his bike for every bit of leverage he could muster, could stay in contact. Evans, Valverde, Andreas Klöden, and Sastre straggled behind, with Levi slotting neatly into their group. The road was lined with fans from Basque, the cycling-mad region of Spain, who dress in orange; the walls of our tunnel vision were colored by them, and the roar of their shouts rolled over us. Alberto slacked his pace slightly, recovered for half a mile, then attacked again.

Rasmussen held his wheel.

I picked up the radio. "Alberto," I said. "Just so you know, Rasmussen told Levi you rode like a little girl yesterday."

A pause. Alberto's voice, angry, came back through the radio: "He'll know what a little girl is today."

I think no one on earth could have stayed with Alberto through the next acceleration. He stood, scooping his feet through the bottom of his pedal strokes, dancing atop his bike and leaping up the hill. Rasmussen fell 50 feet back, 100, 120. His body stiffened; he was no longer rocking on his bike in mere fatigue but teetering on it in exhaustion. I could feel the yellow jersey slipping from his back.

Then, incredibly, somehow Rasmussen began crawling across the gap. Stiff, ungainly, mouth wide, eyes blank, he found Alberto's wheel, and that's how they finished, 5:31 behind stage winner Vino. We had been within a few pedal strokes of cracking Rasmussen.

And that brought us to stage 16. Win or lose. All or nothing
— almost. I had one last chance to change my mind before we got
to the endgame, the mighty Col d'Aubisque.

Carlos Sastre joined the polka-dot-jersey-wearing Mauricio
Soler in an early attack on the first climb of the day, the nine-mile,
HC Port de Larrau. Rasmussen, Alberto, Levi, and Evans let the
move go. By the second of the day's four major climbs, Sastre and
Soler and a few other riders with them had a gap of nearly four and
a half minutes. Soler had started the day fifteen minutes behind
Rasmussen; he was out to secure the polka dot jersey, not a podium
spot. But Sastre could be trouble. He'd started the day in sixth, 6:46
behind Rasmussen, just over a minute behind Levi in fourth and
about three and a half back from Alberto in second. He was, tech-
nically, ahead of Alberto right now — and closing on Rasmussen.

The Rabobank team car — Rasmussen's — pulled up beside me
on the narrow, winding Alpine road.

"Erik!" I yelled out the window to their team director, Erik
Breukink. I knew what he wanted: to work together to chase down
Sastre. If Rabobank and our team went to the front, we'd pull Sastre back easily. He asked if we'd cooperate. "You've got second and
fourth preserved then," Breukink said as he ended his request.

I'd raced with Erik back on ONCE, and for two years on Rabobank, and I respected him. He'd finished third in the 1990 Tour de
France, and won the white jersey in 1988. Since he'd retired and
taken over Rabobank, his team had won Paris-Tours, Milan–San
Remo, the Tour of Spain, and a lot of other races. He was good at
his job. And his offer made a lot of sense. It was the smart thing to
do — what I would have done in his place.

"Sorry, Erik," I said. I smiled. "We're going for the win today."

I was going to force Rasmussen and Rabobank to do all the
chasing on their own, even if it meant we never caught Sastre and
it cost us any chance at a podium spot.

By the time we went up and over the third climb, the Col de
Marie-Blanque, Rabobank's pace had whittled the yellow-jersey
group down to just fifteen riders. By the time we hit the base of the

Aubisque, we could see the break in front of us, forty seconds at the most.

"Patience," I said quietly into the ears of Alberto and Levi and Popo, for even here I knew we would have to wait, that Rasmussen could only be cracked, if at all, at the very end of the end. The Aubisque rewards those who can resist its early, gentler slopes. It climbs up out of a green valley with a cool stream, the Valentine, running alongside. There are chalets, stores, patisseries, fountains where dogs and children alike drink. Then in the last six miles it steepens, shoots up out of civilization, and grows hot and distant. The road winds around far curves, then identically around the next far curve, again and again, so that you can lose your mind, thinking you are pedaling as futilely as a man chasing the horizon. It was then that we would attack.

Seven miles from the summit, I said, "Popo."

He rose from his saddle, pedaled to the front of the group, then sat down and began grinding away at his bike as if it were a monster that was trying to drag him below the surface of the road. Only four of the world's best bicycle riders were able to hang on to his wheel: Alberto, Rasmussen, Evans, and Levi. They rode up to and around Soler, who could not stay with them, then Sastre. With six miles to go, Popo pulled off.

And Levi attacked.

It was a beautiful, spontaneous move made on guts and instinct. He'd been saving himself the entire Tour—originally for the purpose of riding his way onto the podium through attrition. But now he was burning himself to nothing for a teammate. Rasmussen caught his wheel and I said into the radio, "Tunnel coming."

In another mile, I knew, there was a landslide shelter built over the road. I wanted Alberto to attack out of its darkness. When I shouted into his ear, he burst out of the black mouth of the tunnel and I hoped that for Rasmussen, emerging back into the blinding sun with a rider flying away from him, it would feel like a nightmare.

Alberto was away. He had a gap.

This was it.

But Rasmussen ever so slowly closed the distance—it was like watching a minute hand move toward the top of a clock. You could not quite see him gaining but you could not miss the gain. After a quarter-mile, he was back on Alberto's wheel. Evans was still hanging on, dragging himself along on sheer doggedness, refusing to let go of whoever's wheel happened to be last in that elite line.

And I shouted, "Levi!"

Levi rose from his bike though I knew everything in him just wanted to sit at this point. But he drove himself into his pedals and surged forward. Rasmussen immediately covered the move.

I gave them a few seconds. I didn't want the rhythm of attacks to be too predictable. At this point I had to keep my directions simple: their brains would be shutting down, their bodies operated by nothing more than that primitive impulse to triumph over whatever was in front of them. So I said only "Go! Now!"

Even in this state of duress, Alberto Contador can ride a bicycle on a mountain more beautifully than anyone else I have ever seen. If you watched hard you could see that his chest looked as if it were ready to pop, and his head was hanging sideways. But the motion of his legs never faltered. Looking as if he was doing nothing more than sprinting up his driveway at the end of a ride, he pulled away from Rasmussen again.

Levi fell away. Rasmussen wrestled his bike up to Alberto— then attacked, and Evans was swept backward by gravity and exhaustion. Levi, somehow, rode his way to the front again and began making tempo, setting up his teammate once more.

But it was Rasmussen who jumped from the group of three, in the final half-mile, flying away, Levi trailing behind, and Alberto, empty at last, able to do nothing but keep spinning and wait for the end to come.

We had lost the Tour de France.

That night I did something I've never done before: I celebrated a loss.

While the team sat somber at the dinner tables, I ordered two bottles of champagne. When I had a glass in my hand, I stood and raised it and said, "I wanted to say that to win is impossible for us now, as you each know." Rasmussen was 3:10 ahead of Alberto, a gap we could never make up now on the flat stages and in the one time trial left; Levi was in fourth, at 5:59, but just fifty-three seconds behind Evans; if he rode the time trial of his life, he could take third. That would give us two podium spots, Alberto's stage win, and the white jersey—a great year for any team. But not what I had wanted.

"We have reason to be disappointed," I said. "But I'm proud that . . ." I looked at each of them. We had blown ourselves up, but survived. "I'm so proud that we were willing to lose everything for a chance to win."

I hadn't quite known what I was going to say until it came out of my mouth, and I was both a little surprised to hear it and a little surprised at the instant realization that it was true: I was still willing to risk losing to win. Something inside me would never settle for being in the middle. After all those years of dominating the race, it was a good thing to know about myself.

The knowledge almost seemed worth the cost. Almost.

Later that evening, after the riders had gone up to their rooms, I was sitting in the restaurant, talking to a journalist, when he got a call. When he answered his phone, his mouth fell open. He listened for a moment, then put the phone down near his chest and said to me, "Rasmussen has been sent home by his team."

I started to register sadness—for the sport, for the fans, even for Rasmussen himself—then in the next instant, before I could fully feel the emotion, I knew I had to get to Alberto. I went to his room and knocked on the door. Benjamin Noval, his roommate, opened the door and I stepped in.

Alberto was on the phone, talking to his girlfriend.

"Hang up," I said.

I told him all that I knew—that Rabobank had withdrawn

Rasmussen from the Tour after a credible report surfaced that he'd been spotted training in the Dolomites, in Italy, when he'd supposedly been in Mexico, which was one of his excuses for missing the out-of-competition tests.

Alberto said, "I don't want it." By the rules of the Tour, the yellow jersey would be passed to him.

"I know," I said. "I knew you wouldn't." We looked at each other. I said, "But we have it."

"I would rather be second than first this way."

But there was nothing we could do about it; you can't give back time. We were ahead of the 148 other riders left in the Tour de France, by less than two minutes at the closest, and by nearly four hours at the most distant. That didn't mean we had to be in yellow, though. We agreed at that instant that Alberto would not wear the jersey that just a few hours earlier we had been willing to sacrifice everything for.

There would be no yellow jersey for stage 17. No one would wear it. At the end of that stage, someone would be in first — whether it was Alberto or Evans or Levi or Sastre or Valverde or even Soler or Jens Voigt, who was thirty-fourth at 1:17 down, or Cédric Vasseur, who was in fifty-eighth two hours back, or anybody who had ridden, who had started the race and ridden the stage and ended it with less accumulated time than everyone else. That was all Alberto and I could think; that was all that made the thought of wearing the yellow jersey bearable.

In time, I would come to understand that while daily the race had exploded around us, we had outlasted those who had fallen from it the same as if they had cracked, or crashed and broken their legs, or simply, as happens, ceded to a stronger team. Like Levi deliberately pacing inside the pack, we had made no mistakes. I understood that not only is it not the victor's duty to apologize for a win, it is not even his right. A win is a win and you cannot excuse yourself from it because of circumstance. Your opponent's condition is not your fault, nor are their strategies. Rain, heat, the good luck to not get a flat tire, a dog running across the road — none of

tion blasting back through the pack had knocked Jalabert to the pavement. This was before the teamwide use of radios, and none of us saw him crash. He rode in alone, fifty seconds behind, and lost the jersey.

We also had perennial contender Alex Zülle in the hunt for the overall win. I was riding my heart out while never turning my brain off; it was what I did best.

By the end of stage 6, Jalabert was just eight seconds out of yellow again. The next day, the peloton was scheduled to ride 126 miles from Charleroi, France, to Liège, Belgium. My homeland! I knew those roads intimately, with the thoroughness a child has for his neighborhood—every odd little nook, every bump, every turn. The roads were tight and tough and windblown, and although some prerace reports called it a flat stage I knew the route was studded with short, steep climbs.

For an all-around Tour contender, Jalabert was a formidable sprinter. If he could win some of the time-bonus sprints along the way, he could easily make up those eight seconds. The rest of us had to keep the race hard and fast, especially on the sharp hills, to try to shed some of the sprinters who might challenge Jalabert. If possible, we also wanted to let just the right breakaway escape for a win—a small group made up only of riders far behind Jalabert. If everything went right, he'd be back in yellow at the end of the day.

At the start, the sun fell onto our shoulders as if the heat were bags of cement we had to carry—which, as far as I was concerned, was perfect. Anything that made the day harder for the pack was good. Our team was attacking the road like a string of firecrackers, the next one of us going off as soon as the previous attempt went up in smoke. We didn't care so much that our attacks failed and our breakaways were brought back; we just wanted to keep the speed high and wear the pack out. Before the bonus sprints, we'd assemble into a solid line of speed and fling Jalabert up ahead of his rivals. By the last bonus, the first part of our plan had worked. Jalabert became what's known as "the leader on the road." This meant that, although someone else was wearing the yellow jersey, Jalabert currently had the lowest time.

the infinite and unpredictable conditions of competition are yours to feel bad about. To do so dishonors those you defeated.

Of course the Tour de France was not over yet. There was still the 34.5-mile time trial the day before the race ended in Paris.

Cadel Evans, who was 1:50 behind Alberto, was a far better time trialist and could conceivably take the yellow jersey away from us. He'd have to gain more than 30 seconds every ten miles, which I calculated could only happen if Alberto crashed or I let him blow up. It was just like guiding Lance through his bonk on the climb of Joux-Plane: We didn't have to worry about losing 30 seconds, or 60 seconds, or even 109 seconds. All we had to do was ride fast enough to not lose all 110 seconds of our lead.

But just to be sure, I recruited a little extra inspiration.

"Okay, Alberto," I said into the radio once he'd gone down the start ramp for the time trial and I'd pulled the car in behind him. "Calm."

"GO!" screamed a voice from the seat beside me.

I looked over at Lance Armstrong and smiled.

"Can you believe it?" Lance said to me. "Can you believe it, Johan? You better believe it."

And I did, finally, punching our team car through that old, familiar wall of human bodies and sound, the yellow jersey that belonged to our team curved over a speeding bicycle in front of us.

"50 k," I said to Alberto. "*Tranquilo,* man. Don't blow up."

"GIVE IT ALL!" screamed Lance.

And that's how it went, me feeding tranquillity and the calculations of our split times to Alberto while Lance went nuts. I looked in the rearview mirror once and our mechanic had his hands over his ears. It felt perfect. Evans was eating into our lead, but it wasn't going to matter. Behind him, Levi was having the ride of his life, scorching across the streets on his way to a stage win. I was grinning like a buffoon, like a madman, like a victorious Tour de France team director.

"There's a tailwind," I said to Lance, sticking my hand out the window. We both knew that that was a good thing: the faster everyone went, the less time anyone could gain.

"Tailwind," I said into the radio.

"GO! GO! YOU!" screamed Lance as Alberto swooped around a corner.

I thought back to something Lance had said to me once during one of those many discussions we had in 2004 about how many Tours he wanted to win: "The dream is to win as much as you can and still be able to quit as a winner," he'd said, and it had always stuck with me. "That's the art of it, Johan, being perfect."

There in the car, with the former champion beside me and the future champion in front of me, that was the moment I knew.

I knew that when Alberto Contador crossed the line he was going to be assured of winning the Tour de France after the next day's largely ceremonial ride. (The last stage is really only raced once the peloton reaches the Champs Élysées in Paris, and then only among the sprinters.) I knew we were going to have a hell of a party in Paris the next night. I knew that the champion of many Tours de France to come had arrived. I knew that I was a winner. And I knew, finally, after all this time, that I was going to call Eva Maria and Victoria and tell them that I was coming home—that it was time for me, like Lance, to quit as a winner.

17

Winning Leads to Winning

From the smallest victory at home to the most public triumph, every win of your life might be the one that really ends up meaning something.

THERE ARE NO SHORTCUTS to being a winner. I words, to own the yellow jersey on the top step of the in Paris seven years in a row, it took seven years of u sacrifice, of unwavering focus, of total devotion and mania power. To lose it for a year, then own it again, did not m more years' worth of work. It was nine years in the making

And all those years of work don't stand alone, eithe nine years can be traced back to a mere twenty-one pedal took in 1995—less than ten seconds of my life.

Everything Lance, Alberto, and I accomplished was b foundation of smaller achievements, little victories that in us and changed us, that interlocked in ways none of us co foreseen or imagined, yet paved our road to the top.

It was the last year Miguel Indurain would win the Tour d 1995, and my team was fighting desperately to keep it fr pening. We'd already gotten into yellow and lost it on Laurent Jalabert got caught in a crazy crash right before of stage 4; an overeager rider had blown straight throug and into the metal crowd barriers at 30 mph, and the ch the infinite and unpredictable conditions of competition are yours to feel bad about. To do so dishonors those you defeated.

Of course the Tour de France was not over yet. There was still the 34.5-mile time trial the day before the race ended in Paris.

Cadel Evans, who was 1:50 behind Alberto, was a far better time trialist and could conceivably take the yellow jersey away from us. He'd have to gain more than 30 seconds every ten miles, which I calculated could only happen if Alberto crashed or I let him blow up. It was just like guiding Lance through his bonk on the climb of Joux-Plane: We didn't have to worry about losing 30 seconds, or 60 seconds, or even 109 seconds. All we had to do was ride fast enough to not lose all 110 seconds of our lead.

But just to be sure, I recruited a little extra inspiration.

"Okay, Alberto," I said into the radio once he'd gone down the start ramp for the time trial and I'd pulled the car in behind him. "Calm."

"GO!" screamed a voice from the seat beside me.

I looked over at Lance Armstrong and smiled.

"Can you believe it?" Lance said to me. "Can you believe it, Johan? You better believe it."

And I did, finally, punching our team car through that old, familiar wall of human bodies and sound, the yellow jersey that belonged to our team curved over a speeding bicycle in front of us.

"50 k," I said to Alberto. "*Tranquilo*, man. Don't blow up."

"GIVE IT ALL!" screamed Lance.

And that's how it went, me feeding tranquillity and the calculations of our split times to Alberto while Lance went nuts. I looked in the rearview mirror once and our mechanic had his hands over his ears. It felt perfect. Evans was eating into our lead, but it wasn't going to matter. Behind him, Levi was having the ride of his life, scorching across the streets on his way to a stage win. I was grinning like a buffoon, like a madman, like a victorious Tour de France team director.

"There's a tailwind," I said to Lance, sticking my hand out the window. We both knew that that was a good thing: the faster everyone went, the less time anyone could gain.

"Tailwind," I said into the radio.

"GO! GO! YOU!" screamed Lance as Alberto swooped around a corner.

I thought back to something Lance had said to me once during one of those many discussions we had in 2004 about how many Tours he wanted to win: "The dream is to win as much as you can and still be able to quit as a winner," he'd said, and it had always stuck with me. "That's the art of it, Johan, being perfect."

There in the car, with the former champion beside me and the future champion in front of me, that was the moment I knew.

I knew that when Alberto Contador crossed the line he was going to be assured of winning the Tour de France after the next day's largely ceremonial ride. (The last stage is really only raced once the peloton reaches the Champs Élysées in Paris, and then only among the sprinters.) I knew we were going to have a hell of a party in Paris the next night. I knew that the champion of many Tours de France to come had arrived. I knew that I was a winner. And I knew, finally, after all this time, that I was going to call Eva Maria and Victoria and tell them that I was coming home — that it was time for me, like Lance, to quit as a winner.

17

Winning Leads to Winning

From the smallest victory at home to the most public triumph, every win of your life might be the one that really ends up meaning something.

THERE ARE NO SHORTCUTS to being a winner. In other words, to own the yellow jersey on the top step of the podium in Paris seven years in a row, it took seven years of unending sacrifice, of unwavering focus, of total devotion and maniacal willpower. To lose it for a year, then own it again, did not mean two more years' worth of work. It was nine years in the making. See?

And all those years of work don't stand alone, either. Those nine years can be traced back to a mere twenty-one pedal strokes I took in 1995 — less than ten seconds of my life.

Everything Lance, Alberto, and I accomplished was built on a foundation of smaller achievements, little victories that influenced us and changed us, that interlocked in ways none of us could have foreseen or imagined, yet paved our road to the top.

It was the last year Miguel Indurain would win the Tour de France, 1995, and my team was fighting desperately to keep it from happening. We'd already gotten into yellow and lost it once, when Laurent Jalabert got caught in a crazy crash right before the finish of stage 4; an overeager rider had blown straight through a turn and into the metal crowd barriers at 30 mph, and the chain reaction blasting back through the pack had knocked Jalabert to the pavement. This was before the teamwide use of radios, and none of us saw him crash. He rode in alone, fifty seconds behind, and lost the jersey.

We also had perennial contender Alex Zülle in the hunt for the overall win. I was riding my heart out while never turning my brain off; it was what I did best.

By the end of stage 6, Jalabert was just eight seconds out of yellow again. The next day, the peloton was scheduled to ride 126 miles from Charleroi, France, to Liège, Belgium. My homeland! I knew those roads intimately, with the thoroughness a child has for his neighborhood—every odd little nook, every bump, every turn. The roads were tight and tough and windblown, and although some prerace reports called it a flat stage I knew the route was studded with short, steep climbs.

For an all-around Tour contender, Jalabert was a formidable sprinter. If he could win some of the time-bonus sprints along the way, he could easily make up those eight seconds. The rest of us had to keep the race hard and fast, especially on the sharp hills, to try to shed some of the sprinters who might challenge Jalabert. If possible, we also wanted to let just the right breakaway escape for a win—a small group made up only of riders far behind Jalabert. If everything went right, he'd be back in yellow at the end of the day.

At the start, the sun fell onto our shoulders as if the heat were bags of cement we had to carry—which, as far as I was concerned, was perfect. Anything that made the day harder for the pack was good. Our team was attacking the road like a string of firecrackers, the next one of us going off as soon as the previous attempt went up in smoke. We didn't care so much that our attacks failed and our breakaways were brought back; we just wanted to keep the speed high and wear the pack out. Before the bonus sprints, we'd assemble into a solid line of speed and fling Jalabert up ahead of his rivals. By the last bonus, the first part of our plan had worked. Jalabert became what's known as "the leader on the road." This meant that, although someone else was wearing the yellow jersey, Jalabert currently had the lowest time.

Still we attacked, over and over and over. My lungs felt as if someone had poured kerosene down my throat and tossed a lit match in my mouth. Around me, I could see leg muscles quivering, jerseys soaked through with sweat. White lines of salt ringed mouths. Eyes were glassy. *All in all, just another day at the office,* I thought, and right then we came up onto a sharp hill I knew called Mont Theux, and I rose out of the saddle and threw myself at it as if I were trying to bore a hole through it rather than ride over it.

Even compared to the hard efforts we'd been making all day, this one hurt. A bunch of riders clattered up the road with me, starting fast then slowing as we rolled up the hill. As soon as I noticed the hesitation, I attacked again — I wanted to make the whole race chase me.

I could feel guys behind me, latching on, sticking their wheels in my draft, then peeling away and being whisked backward. I never glanced behind me — I wanted them to think I was looking all the way to Liège, thirty miles or so away. But through a change in air pressure or subtle variations in the shadows cast on the road, or some other subconscious clue, I could sense the riders one by one being sucked away from me and back toward the pack.

Then I was all alone, out in front of the Tour de France.

I put my head down and pedaled.

Back in the pack, unknown to me, at about the same time I was riding off the front of my breakaway, Big Mig Indurain was rising out of the saddle and starting to turn the cranks of his bike with frightening force. He passed by the front of the pack as if they were hitchhikers sticking out their thumbs, and rocketed into the gap between me and the peloton.

Indurain was often criticized for the way he won his five Tours de France. With some variation through the years, he would mark the climbers in the mountains and crush the entire field in the time trials. In general, his reign was characterized by unyielding dominance rather than legendary exploits and thrilling attacks. He was not a volcano; he was, rather, its comparatively sedate yet unstoppable lava flow.

Occasionally, this reputation would seem to rankle Indurain, or else maybe he found strategic value in delivering sporadic reminders that though he preferred to win simply by leading the pack, he could also tear it to shreds. Whatever had happened, Indurain was on the attack.

A Tour de France pack is made up of the top 1 percent of the top 1 percent of bicycle racers in the world. There are multiple world champions, legends any direction you care to look, prodigies — it is unlike any other bicycle race. And from that pack full of the champions of champions, only a single rider was able to scratch his way into Indurain's draft, a racer from the Polti team.

When Indurain came by me it was as if a train had passed — in literal, actual fact that is how I perceived it. There was a great outward movement of air as he pushed the atmosphere out of his way, then a whooshing noise and the big, steaming locomotive of his body streaming by. I blurred my feet in ever-faster circles and when the gasping rider behind him passed me as well, I kicked myself sideways into their combined draft.

Sometimes for training, professional racers do something called motorpacing. A scooter or motorcycle drives directly in front of us, pulling us along for miles and miles at 35 to 45 mph. It teaches your body how to handle the stress of turning over your biggest gear and operating at the speed, while eliminating the need to overcome the wind resistance. I felt as if I was motorpacing behind Indurain.

I stuck my head out into the wind, and I saw another climb that I knew, Côte des Forges. It was extremely steep, and I was glad to see it, because it meant we'd get a break — Indurain would have to slow down. To get up the hill, we would have to shift our chains from the biggest chain ring up front down onto the smaller chain ring, which made pedaling easier.

We shot toward the hill and I kept waiting for him to shift down. We hit the base and our front wheels pointed up, and still he didn't shift down. Indurain rose out of the saddle and jackhammered his pedals, but he didn't shift. I gritted my teeth and pushed against my pedals with as much force as I could — it was like jumping on concrete. My bones rattled inside. I needed to shift to my little ring, but I refused to. I thought to myself, *If Indurain doesn't shift, I won't shift.* The Polti rider with us made the shift—and disappeared like something we'd thrown overboard.

I must have made it to the top of that climb, because I was on a flat road again and I could hear Indurain saying something to me. He softened the battering of his pedals and I steered to the left, then pulled up beside him.

"Work with me," Indurain said.

"I can't," I said, and he knew why: with Jalabert and Zülle on my team, I could not help Indurain gain any time on the pack. All I could do was follow him. Race tactics are often cruel. To stay away from the pack—and gain time on his rivals—Indurain would have to be willing to ride as hard as he could while I did nothing more than draft behind him. We each knew that meant I was more likely to arrive at the finish line fresher, with more energy and a better chance to win the stage.

The problem for me was, drafting behind him was not a given. We still had about ten miles to go, and I wasn't sure I could hold Indurain's speed. I reached out with my right hand and tapped his butt and pushed him forward.

And my immolation continued.

Liège is Belgium's third-biggest city, and when Indurain and I stormed through its limits it seemed as if the entire population had come out to see the race—fans were standing four, five, six, ten deep in places, hanging over the metal crowd-control barriers and screaming wildly to see a Belgian on the wheel of the Tour's champion. Indurain was riding hard against the barriers, first on the far left side of the road then the left, tacking across the pavement in ferocious arcs to set up for each twist and turn of the city streets. He was staying close to the crowd to hide from the wind—and so he had to watch only one side for my eventual attack.

The speed he was maintaining was phenomenal. I was doing my best to concentrate on not wasting energy—dodging around be-

hind him to always find the best draft, monitoring myself to make
sure my elbows were loose, my shoulders not hunched, my jaw not
clenched. Every so often I'd reach down and pluck the red water
bottle from its cage and sneak in a quick drink.

We passed under a huge, inflatable arch that announced we had
one kilometer to go—about half a mile. Belgian flags flapped in
our faces, hung over the barriers by fans. Indurain was hunched
over, working at his pedals still with that same monstrous fluidity, and I looked down at my own, comparatively thin legs and realized I must look willowy hiding behind him. Yet I was there, and
the cheers were for me.

Motorcycles and cars rumbled close behind us, the TV cameras
and race officials, the VIPs and neutral support mechanics piling
up behind us to get a glimpse of the finish.

I could still hear my chain going round and round, round and
round. I could hear breath entering my lungs, rushing back out
of my mouth. My heart thumped against the inside of my chest. I
cocked my head to the right, trying to see past the locomotive in
front of me. I tucked back in hard behind Indurain and noticed it,
then, his race number, pinned onto his jersey: number 1. Given to
the winner of the previous Tour de France.

Number 1. As if it were mocking me. Who was I to think I could
beat number 1?

We sliced left through a turn, and Indurain was out of the saddle. The roar of the crowd was like an avalanche of noise bury-
ing us. His hands were in the curved drops of the handlebar and,
standing in an angry hunch he leveraged each arm and its oppos-
ing leg against each other, nearly bending his bike sideways with
every pedal stroke, the full tremendous power of his body going
into the bike and shooting him forward.

I couldn't believe it. After all this time, after all these miles, he
could sprint like this.

I shook my head, then whipped my feet into a frenzy and accelerated straight up into the gap Indurain's burst had opened—I
charged at his rear wheel as if I were a battering ram. At the last
instant before we collided I jerked my hips left and the bike swept

out to the side. Because I'd accelerated in the quiet draft behind him, even after I left the shelter of his body and hit the wind myself I was already moving faster than Indurain.

I passed him.

I could see the finish banner.

I took the first of those twenty-one pedal strokes.

Call it ten seconds. I don't know for sure. At sprint speed in the Tour de France, figure two full pedal strokes a second, 120 rpm. It took me ten complete revolutions to get in front of Indurain.

He threw his bike left, diving behind me—everything reversed now, the great champion hoping to use my draft. I looked over my shoulder to see if he'd been able to tuck in, and that was three pedal strokes. He was in. That was bad.

I looked forward, but I remember I didn't really see the finish line. I just didn't want to have to look at Indurain anymore. I dropped my head down and tried to release my legs from the puny bounds of my body. I needed them to do what I could not. My shoulders came forward and my head dropped farther—I was instinctively trying to become a wedge, an aerodynamic shape, slippery to the air that sought to hold me back. Yet my elbows flapped wildly. I was trying to put power into the pedals with every part of my body; I wouldn't be surprised in some way if in my desperation I'd figured out how to pedal with my eyelids, with my hair and fingernails.

That was seventeen pedal strokes.

I was still in front of Indurain. Through the blur of my legs and the yellow frame of my bike, I could see him behind me.

I raised my head. That was twenty pedal strokes.

I took the twenty-first pedal stroke, then I won.

On Sunday, July 29, 2007, about four hours after Alberto Contador became the champion of the 94th Tour de France, we held a party for three hundred people—family and friends—at La Maison Blanche in Paris. There were speeches and videos and music and an ocean of champagne, and I found myself next to Alberto

Contador, Tour de France champion. I hugged him. I said, "You cannot realize what you have done."

I think I might have sounded like somebody's crotchety old grandfather, talking to a twenty-four-year-old kid. But I kept going. Perhaps it was the champagne. I said, "Life will never be the same for you anymore."

"I know," said Alberto, stepping back and putting a hand on my shoulder as if he were trying to comfort me. "I know. I know."

But he didn't. He couldn't. None of us ever can know where our next win will take us.

Lance Armstrong, Alberto Contador, and I had created something perfect. Between the three of us, we had won the greatest sporting event in the world seven times, then lost once to make it known how precious and unlikely that next win was, before going out the very next chance we had and taking it. I had been moving this way for quite some time—for sure since Lance had started talking of retirement—but until Alberto finally secured the yellow jersey I hadn't known for sure that my goal was not to just keep on winning as many Tours as I could. I wanted to end it all at the right time. I wanted that thing we had all created—our team—to stay perfect forever, to not go on to win some more, then lose some, then have trouble finding a sponsor someday, then someday be hit by a scandal and reorganize and come back and win some more and lose some more and just become one more cycling team.

Cycling is my life. For twenty-five years all I have known is bike racing, and I doubt that I can ever leave it. But I had won that victory that would let me find my way back to my wife and daughter. Whatever jobs or chances I take in the future, there will be more time for me to be a father and husband.

I had won enough to quit as a winner with the team Lance and I built. And so had he: when I told him I was resigning, we agreed to disband the team. Nothing can ever touch the purity of what we accomplished now. Nothing can ever change it. We turned it into a monument—to hope, belief, heart, victory.

. . .

I took that twenty-first pedal stroke, and I won the stage. I won the yellow jersey.

I'd end up wearing it for just one day. Indurain would take it the next day in the time trial, and though Zülle and Jalabert would fight hard, each of them winning one of the upcoming mountain stages, the greatest Spanish rider of our generation would wear yellow all the way to Paris once he put it on.

On the podium in Liège, the King of Belgium, Albert the Third, shook my hand and said, "This is a great day for Belgium."

I thanked him. I also agreed with him. "Yes," I said. "This is a great day."

But I really had no idea how great of a day it was — back there in the heat of the stage, when I'd made that first withering attack on the hill, something had happened that would end up meaning far more to me than that yellow jersey.

Rider after rider had tried to stay with me, and one by one they'd peeled off and gone flapping back down the road in the wind. The last bicycle racer to stay with me before I got away, the most stubborn of all the ones who'd chased me, and the angriest about not being able to hold my wheel, was a twenty-three-year-old kid who showed great promise but had yet to even finish a Tour de France. Lance Armstrong never forgot how I rode him off my wheel that day and pedaled away to steal a yellow jersey from one of the great champions of the Tour de France.

I had my victories as a bike racer, but they were hardscrabble wins — torn away tooth and nail (and brain) from those who possessed vastly more physical gifts than I. Taken on its own, my entire racing career would be reduced by now to nothing but a few quirky footnotes beloved by fanatics: won what was then the fastest stage of the Tour de France, rode off a cliff, was the only rider who held Indurain's wheel in the legendary 1995 attack. But I happened to triumph in a few key wins that impressed themselves upon a kid who spoke with a Texas twang and understood just a little about bike racing.

Lance likes to remind me that he'd crashed just a few days before that stage in 1995 and was feeling bad—or else, he says, he'd easily have been able to stick with me.

"Come on, Johan," he jokes, gesturing to his legs, his power-house lungs, the heart of a superhero. "I mean, take a look. You think you could ride away from this?"

One day I told him he was lucky he hadn't kept up.

"What are you talking about?" he said.

"If that hadn't left such an impression," I said, "if I hadn't been able to pop you off my wheel and finish three minutes in front of you, bandages or not, you just might have picked a different team director all those years later."

You never know which moment of success will be the one that ends up changing your life, so they're all worth fighting for. From the smallest victory at home to the most public triumph, every win of your life might be the one that really ends up meaning some-thing, that transforms you from simply the winner of the moment into that rarest thing of all: a true winner.

APPENDIX

Johan Bruyneel's Cycling Career

Riding Career

TEAMS

SEFB	1989
Lotto	1990–1991
ONCE	1992–1995
Rabobank	1997
ONCE	1998

VICTORIES

1988
Izegem
Tour de la CEE, stage 1

1989
Berlare
Flèche Nieloise
Tour de la CEE, stage 7
Tour of Switzerland, stage 2
Tour of Switzerland, stage 10
Wavre

1990
Herselt
Tour de la CEE

Tour de l'Avenir
Tour du Vaucluse, stage 3

1991
Critérium de Geraardsbergen
Grand Prix de Frankfurt
Grand Prix du Midi Libre, stage 3
Tour du Pays Basque, stage 5

1992
Coppa Placci
Grand Prix des Nations
Rund um den Henninger Turm
Tour of Spain, stage 12

1993
Critérium de Geraardsbergen
Semaine Catalane
Tour de France, stage 6

1994
Boland Bank Tour, stage 3
Tour de la Rioja, stage 4

1995
Critérium d'Alost
Grand Prix du Midi Libre, stage 5
Tour de France, stage 7

1996
Critérium de Peer
Hofbrau Cup, stage 3

1997
Flèche Manuroise

Team Director Career

TEAMS

U.S. Postal Service   1999–2004
Discovery Channel   2005–2007

VICTORIES

1999

Circuit de la Sarthe, stage 4 (Lance)
Dauphiné Libéré, prologue (Lance)
First Union Classic
Four Days of Dunkirk, best young rider
Redlands Classic
Route de Sud, stage 4 (Lance)
Tour de France
Tour de France, prologue
Tour de France, stage 8
Tour de France, stage 9
Tour de France, stage 19

2000

Grand Prix Eddy Merckx
Tour de France
Tour de France, stage 19

2001

Ghent-Wevelgem
Tour de France
Tour de France, stage 10
Tour de France, stage 11
Tour de France, stage 18

2002

Tour de France
Tour de France, stage 11

Tour de France, stage 12
Tour de France, stage 19
U.S. National Road Championship
Vuelta a Murcia

2003
Tour de France
Tour de France, stage 4
Tour de France, stage 15
Tour of Spain
Tour of Spain, stage 20

2004
Three Days of De Panne
Tour de France
Tour de France, stage 4
Tour de France, stage 13
Tour de France, stage 15
Tour de France, stage 16
Tour de France, stage 17
Tour de France, stage 19
Tour de Georgia
Tour de Georgia, stage 3
Tour de Georgia, stage 4

2005
Dauphiné Libéré, points classification
Dauphiné Libéré, prologue
Dauphiné Libéré, stage 7
Dauphiné Libéré, team classification
Eneco Tour of Benelux, stage 1
Eneco Tour of Benelux, stage 5
Giro d'Italia
Giro d'Italia, stage 11
GP Ouest-France
Hervis Tour of Australia, team classification

Tour de France

Tour de France, best young rider

Tour de France, stage 4

Tour de France, stage 15

Tour de France, stage 17

Tour de France, stage 20

Tour de Georgia

Tour de Georgia, stage 5

Tour of Spain, stage 6

Volta a Catalunya

2006

Belgium National Time Trial Championship

Deutschland Tour, best young rider

Deutschland Tour, prologue

Eneco Tour of Benelux, stage 4

Giro d'Italia, combination classification

Giro d'Italia, prologue

Hervis Tour of Austria

Japan National Road Championship

Japan National Time Trial Championship

Sachen Tour International

Three Days of De Panne

Three Days of De Panne, King of the Mountains

Three Days of De Panne, stage 1

Three Days of De Panne, stage 4

Tour de France, stage 12

Tour de Pologne, stage 1

Tour de Romandie, prologue

Tour of California, stage 2

Tour of California, stage 5

Tour of Spain, King of the Mountains

Tour of Spain, stage 11

Tour of Spain, stage 17

Tour of Spain, team classification

United Kingdom National Cyclo-Cross Championship
U.S. National Road Championship

2007

Belgian National Road Championship
Paris-Nice
Paris-Nice, best young rider
Paris-Nice, stage 4
Paris-Nice, stage 5
Paris-Nice, stage 7
Russian National Time Trial Championship
Three Days of De Panne, stage 4
Tour de France
Tour de France, best young rider
Tour de France, stage 14
Tour de France, stage 19
Tour de France, team classification
Tour de Georgia
Tour de Georgia, best young rider
Tour de Georgia, stage 3
Tour de Georgia, stage 4
Tour de Georgia, stage 5
Tour de Georgia, team classification
Tour de l'Ain, stage 2
Tour de Suisse, mountains classification
Tour de Suisse, stage 6
Tour of Austria
Tour of Austria, stage 5
Tour of Austria, stage 7
Tour of Belgium
Tour of Belgium, stage 3
Tour of California
Tour of California, prologue
Tour of California, stage 5
Tour of Missouri

Tour of Missouri, stage 2

Tour of Missouri, stage 3

Tour of Qinghai Lake, points classification

Tour of Qinghai Lake, stage 1

Tour of Qinghai Lake, stage 3

Tour of Qinghai Lake, stage 5

Tour of Qinghai Lake, stage 6

Tour of Qinghai Lake, stage 8

Tour of Qinghai Lake, stage 9

Tour of Spain, stage 14

U.S. National Road Championship

Volta a Catalunya, stage 3

Vuelta a la Comunidad Valenciana, stage 4

Vuelta a Mallorca, metas volantes

Vuelta Ciclista a Castilla y León

Vuelta Ciclista a Castilla y León, combination classification

Vuelta Ciclista a Castilla y León, Spanish rider classification

Vuelta Ciclista a Castilla y León, stage 4

ACKNOWLEDGMENTS

The number of people who contribute to a single victory, let alone those who helped me to eight Tour de France wins and all those who influenced me throughout my amateur and pro careers, is literally countless to me. No one wins alone, at least not in cycling, or life.

Rather than attempting to name that multitude and risk omitting someone, I send my thanks out to all those I ever competed with or against, was on a team with or worked with as staff, those who provided examples I could study either consciously or not, all those who sponsored the many teams I've been affiliated with, all the fans — the beating heart of cycling — and the many creative and business-oriented people who helped bring my teams, business ventures, and this book to life.

I want each of you to know and to feel that you had a part in my past victories and those to come. Thank you for being winners. Thank you for helping me become one.

INDEX